Putting Their Hands in His

Teaching Children How to Pray

Putting
Their Hands
in His

Ruthie Jacobsen

Personal Applications by Noelene Johnsson

To

Our husbands, Don Jacobsen
& Bill Johnsson,
who are not only loving
and supportive husbands,
but caring and exemplary fathers.

Acknowledgments

Our thanks to many people who have contributed to this book, who have supported and believed.

Thank you to David Ring, who, after reading the manuscript of the first chapter, was gracious and willing to have his story told again here as an encouragement to parents and others. His belief in "singing at midnight" is an inspiration.

Thanks to Don Moen, the composer, and the Integrity Music Company, of Mobile, Alabama, for their permission to use the powerful words of the song, "GOD WILL MAKE A WAY." That song has been used of God in innumerable settings to bring hope and a realization that God's very nature is to hear, to answer prayer, and to bless His family on earth.

Thank you to Nelita Trotman, whose thrilling story is included, with her permission in Chapter one.

Thank you to Diane Baier, whose artist skills and suggestions have helped tremendously. We thank God for her gifts and sweet spirit.

Table of Contents

Introduction

"A wise teacher makes learning a joy."
—Proverbs 15:12, *The Living Bible*

This came from God's Word. Ellen G. White says that Scripture is not just His written Word to us, it is His spoken word to our hearts. We have a mandate from the highest Source to make the learning of prayer a pleasant experience.

We are not so concerned to teach about prayer— prayer is not our goal. Our goal is a *relationship* with God. And prayer is a means to making this connection with Him.

Chapter 1

The Power of a Song

What do you do when the bottom falls out? What do you do when it's midnight in your life? How can you give direction and stability to your children when your life seems to be falling apart? What can your children learn about God in the tough times?

David Ring, the well-known, and much loved evangelist with cerebral palsy, tells in his own inimitable way, about the power of a song in his life, and how he imagines the miracle at Philippi:

It was midnight. Two prisoners were in jail, in stocks - when Paul turned and said, "Silas, do you still have a song left in you?"

"Yup, I think I do," was the answer.

"Just start singing something, and I'll follow." The Bible says that they sang at *midnight*.

David Ring says, "God loves singing! Probably hundreds of times in Scripture we are told to sing."

"What do you do when you've just been given disappointing or discouraging news from your physician? What do you do when your mate walks away? What do you do when you look into the face of a loved one— in a casket? You SING."

"You might say, that's not in the Bible!"

"Oh yes it is! Look at Paul and Silas in the jail in Philippi. The Bible says that their song flooded the jail

—all the prisoners were listening, to two men who could *sing* at midnight! But that song traveled, out into the street, up into the night sky, past the moon, past the stars. That song made its way all the way to heaven and reached the throne room of God, and God heard it.

"And He said, 'Shh, Shh, angels, listen, I hear singing!'

'Of course you do, God. We sing all the time up here!'

"'No, I hear singing from a jail in Philippi, and I *like* it!'

"And God listened, and then He started tapping His foot.

"Now you're going to say, 'Preacher, that is NOT in Scripture!'

"Oh yeah? The Bible says that there was an *earthquake*! What do you think caused the earthquake? God was tapping His foot to their singing, to their music of praise."

The Bible says that they sang at midnight, when things looked completely hopeless. They had been stripped and beaten with rods. In fact, the story says that they were severely beaten and thrown into prison.

"The jailer was ordered to make sure that they didn't escape. So he took no chances but put them into the inner dungeon and clamped their feet in the stocks. Around midnight, Paul and Silas were praying and singing hymns to God and the other prisoners were listening. Suddenly there was a great earthquake and the prison was shaken to its foundations." *Acts 16:23-26 NLT*

As the gospel song says, "Troubles come to us all." What do you do at midnight? How do you teach your children to sing in their darkest hours? By example.

They learn from the models around them. They are affected by the moods, attitudes, atmosphere. They see where you go for help when you're in trouble. They see your strength, faith, and willingness to sing when times are hard. Your example gives them more strength and courage than you may realize.

We're not talking about singing "on stage." This is singing for the ears of God, singing songs of faith, songs of victory, songs of thanksgiving and trust. The power of a song is incalculable. God loves your singing, and He loves to hear your children sing to Him. This is a form of prayer that is powerful because it changes not only you, but it can change circumstances and situations and people around you. As David Ring says, "God likes it." There is power in a song.

Sue Thomas had two great dreams, one was to be able to sing with a group of people who were singing hymns and songs of praise. She longed to sing with performers who knew and loved God. The other dream was for a baby grand piano. But there were some major hurdles in her way. There were impossibilities to her dreams. You see, Sue is deaf. Profoundly deaf.

Some of her first memories of Christmas were of visits to a big, beautiful department store in their city. She remembers, as a small child, when her mother took her into the store to see all the Christmas decorations. It seemed that one store competed with the next for displays and music at Christmas.

Her mother squeezed her hand tightly as they came into the store where the large grand piano commanded attention. It seemed to demand respect and awe.

Then she saw tears streaming down her mother's cheeks because they were surrounded by the glorious music of the Christmas season that her mother loved, and that she knew Sue would never hear. Her parents had dreamed of their only daughter long before she was born, and hoped that one day she would become a musician. They loved music, and wanted her to enjoy it too.

Sue remembers sitting on her mother's lap as her mother sang, "Silent Night, Holy Night, all is calm, all is bright." She would reach her little hands up to her mother's throat to catch all the vibrations she possibly could. This became "her song." She loved it. It never failed to bring her peace. In the deepest parts of her soul she treasured her song. It belonged to her, and she knew that Jesus loved her and had a plan for Sue Thomas. She somehow understood that this Holy Child came to earth to die for her and that song became her strength, a place where she found refuge.

In elementary school she was teased by other children because she "talked funny." She said, "I would punch out the boys for making fun of me, and invariably would find myself in the principal's office for disturbing peace in school." She could never tell anyone how she felt, or what really happened.

After she was punished, she would go back to her desk, and turn her face to the window so no one could see the tears of frustration and hurt, and she would silently sing her song. Sue found peace in Someone Who was there just for her. He understood. There was a place where all was calm—all was bright.

She successfully completed college, and, because of her bright mind and extraordinary ability to read lips, was given some prestigious opportunities. She worked with the FBI and other organizations. Sue became a trusted and competent professional.

Bill Gaither, who has brought musicians together for video and public concerts, invited Sue Thomas to join them and to SING with them! She told her story there that day, and then she sang "Silent Night." Although her melody didn't match the familiar song, it was beautiful, and from her heart. It was *her* song. The rhythm was perfect; only the melody was changed, because Sue has never really heard the melody. But Sue's song, her own interpretation of "Silent Night," was beautiful. Men and women wept as Sue sang a song she had learned from her mother who patiently taught her the song that would change her life. There is power in a song.

From the time that a baby is tiny, there are responses to music. The right music is elevating, and brings hope, encouragement, optimism, joy, and strength that can be found in no other source. Surround your children with good music. Teach them the words and sing together as a family.

At a recent Teen Prayer & Ministry Conference at Union College, a student from England taught the group a song they learned to love and sang over and over throughout the weekend. A few weeks later there was another Teen Prayer & Ministry Conference at Walla Walla College, and Steve and Judy Evenson taught the group the song. Again it became a favorite. Are you curious? Here are the words—not profound, but true, and the young people sang this song with energy and meaning. We could see again, the power of a song:

Jesus, build a fence all around me every day.
Lord, I want you to protect me as I travel along life's way.
Lord, I know You can. Lord, I know You will—
*   fight my battles if I stand still.*
Build a fence, Lord, around me every day.

I met with an interdenominational prayer group in New York and mentioned that little song. They wanted to learn it, so I sang it for them. They kept saying, "Sing it again. Sing it again, one more time."

There is something about a song that God likes. Heaven is filled with music. Ask Him how to share His love with your children through music. Make your worship times and prayers at bedtime happy with songs. Often this will be the very last thought before they go to sleep, and the first thought the next morning.

This morning as I was getting ready to go to the Baltimore airport to catch a plane for California, I was standing in the bathroom brushing my teeth, and was amazed to "hear" a little song in my heart—a song we had sung so often as elementary students—many years ago, at the church school in Milton, Oregon:

"O, the lark sings in the meadow, in the bright and cheery meadow, and a happy song sings he.
And the burden of his trilling, all the air with music filling, it is this: 'God cares for me.'
God cares for me. Bright is the day before me.
Where'er I go, right well I know, His loving care is o'er me!"

What comfort in those words! What a peace! What a powerful truth! Where did this little song come from? I hadn't thought about it or sung it for many years, but it was there, every word still impressed on my mind, and it still had meaning, maybe more meaning now than when we first learned it and sang it so often as children. The power of a song.

Thank God for Christian teachers, Christian parents. Teach your children to sing their prayers to God. He likes it.

David Ring learned the power of a song in a unique and surprising way. He had been visiting churches for 10 years, telling his story, and people were responding. God was changing lives.

But one night, as he stopped by a college in Missouri to pick up his girlfriend, Karen, (who later became his wife,) he thought about his ministry and wanted to do something more to bless the people. As they drove toward the church, he described their conversation something like this:

"Tonight, Babe, I want to do something different. This is a little dinky church in an itsy bitsy town, and maybe they won't know any better. I want to do something to bless the people. Tonight I'm going to *sing.*"

"You're going to do WHAT?" she asked? You see, David can't carry a tune. He cannot follow the melody at all. If it weren't for the words, you may not know what he's singing. But that night he wanted to sing.

At the close of his sermon, he told the congregation what he was going to do. He said, " Now I know that God called me to preach. He didn't call me to sing, and after you hear me tonight, you're going to say, amen, stick to preachin', boy."

Then he told the organist to go to the bench and to play an introduction. He said, "Play this softly, and slowly," and David Ring began to sing ...

> *"I've heard an old, old story—how a Savior came from glory.*
> *How He gave His life on Calvary, to save a wretch like me.*
> *I've heard about His groaning, of His precious life atoning,*
> *And I repented of my sins and won the victory.*

O victory in Jesus, my Savior forever.
He sought me, and bought me with His redeeming blood.
He loved me e'er I knew Him, and all my love is due Him.
He plunged me to victory beneath the cleansing flood.

He looked out over the congregation. There were
about 90 people there that night, and he saw men and
women weeping as they were coming forward to the
altar to give their hearts to God or to renew a commit-
ment to Him. David says, "Somehow I knew—God liked
it." So he sang his favorite verse, which is so full of
meaning for him ...

"'I've heard about His healing, of His precious love revealing
How He made the lame to walk again, and caused the
blind to see.
And then I cried, 'Lord Jesus, come and heal my broken
spirit.'
And somehow Jesus came to me and brought the victory."

As he finished his song that night, in that little town
in Missouri, it seemed that everyone in the church had
come forward. It was a new day for David and for his
ministry. He still can't sing. He still can't carry a tune.
But he has promised God that everywhere he goes,
he's going to sing that song. He has kept his promise,
and God has been faithful in bringing thousands of
people of all ages and cultures to the cross. For 19
years, he has sung that song everywhere he goes.

He said that there have been some times in some very
large churches when he has said to God: "Tonight I'm
not going to sing." But somehow God seemed to say to
him, "Oh yes, you are!"

The arguing went something like this: "God did you
see that huge choir? Everyone in that choir could sing
me under the table." But he knew that God was saying,
"I know that, but just sing, and let me put the choir
under the table."

Because of his disability, his teachers and family—everyone—discouraged him from taking the ministry. But now he has 800 invitations to speak *every year.* He says, "When I get a few more, I'm going to go FULL TIME." Six days every week, he's somewhere speaking, and he says that those in the audience make very real and special commitments to God. It's as though they are saying: "Lord, if you can use *David Ring,* please use me."

We have so many reasons to sing, but probably the most important times to sing are when we don't *feel* like singing. Ask God for a song. Ask Him for a song for your child. There are little songs, big songs, and songs of power. There are songs with warmth and love, cheer, and great encouragement. There are big songs of triumph and hope. Ask Him for specific songs that will lift burdens and bring new light and help to your home and your family.

Not only was Martin Luther not invited to the Diet of Spires—he was told he could not appear. This was a tremendously significant court session when all that he believed, taught, and stood for would be debated, argued, and judged. Who would be there in his defense?

A little group of his fledgling followers were appointed and tried their best to prepare for this awesome assignment, and the more they worked, the more frightened they became. But their great teacher, Luther himself, decided to travel with them as far as possible. So they journeyed together all the way to the city limits of the city of Spires, Germany. As they trudged along together, they worshipped, they studied Scripture, they prayed together, and they sang.

They sang the great anthem of the church—"A Mighty Fortress is our God, a Bulwark, never failing. Our Helper, He, amid the flood, of mortal ills prevailing." This song was given to Martin Luther—*for this trip!* Amazing! God could see their need, and provided for them in this time of emergency. And He provided a *song.* You can almost hear his big German voice booming out those powerful words of the last verse:

> *"Let goods and kindred go. This mortal life also.*
> *The body they may kill. His truth abideth still.*
> *His kingdom is forever."*

In the book, *The Great Controversy,* it says that when his defenders walked into the courtroom the next day they had a totally different frame of mind. Now they weren't fearful and cowering. They walked into that august assembly with their backs straight and their heads held high. They had just been in prayer, and they had sung powerful words of truth. They were now infused with a new sense of hope and purpose. They were prepared by God Himself. No wonder they were not afraid.

Hundreds of times in Scripture we are told, "Don't be afraid" and Luther had been tutoring them from God's Word. He had been singing powerful words, "wonderful words of life," and they were changed. The cause of truth won a mighty victory that day. The power of a song.

Teach your children the words of big songs, even if they don't understand the meaning on an adult level. Those words and the melodies are there—in the computer, and for a lifetime.

David Ring says, "If you're not having a spiritual earthquake, you're not singing. SING."

Dr. JoAnn Davidson, who teaches Theology at the Seminary at Andrews University, tells what she did when their two children were pre-schoolers.

She was looking for ways to make the Sabbath morning church service more relevant for their two little ones.

Each week, she called the church office to find out which hymns would be used for the service the next Sabbath morning, and she would sing those songs as she worked in their home throughout the week.

She didn't always sit down with her children and teach them the words, but they heard the melodies and the words as she did her housework. By the time they were seated together in the pew for the worship service, or standing as the congregation sang the hymns, one of the children might whisper, "Momma, I know that song!" She was making deposits into little memory banks with powerful words.

The power of a song. Teach your children to sing. You may be asking, "How do I do this? When? We're all so busy!"

The Bible says that we should teach our children when we go out and when we come in. How about teaching them songs as you drive to school, or as the family is traveling together on a trip. Teach them the words to a song. Make it a pleasant game, to see who can remember the words.

My friends, Jansen and Gloria Trotman, moved recently to Trinidad, where Pastor Jansen is the President of the Caribbean Union Conference. When they were living in St. Croix, U.S. V. I., Gloria was teaching, and their daughter, Nelita, was a student at the academy there.

One morning as they drove to school together, they were singing a song that Gloria had just learned at Campmeeting in Antigua.

I had been there for Campmeeting, and each morning in a seminar, we talked about different forms of prayer—praise, quietness, listening, confession, singing, etc. When we discussed the topic of singing as a form of prayer, we sang "God Will Make A Way"—a beautiful song by Don Moen. They were learning the song, and since we all loved it, we sang it often during the week.

"God will make a way when there seems to be no way.
He works in ways we cannot see. He will make a way for
    me.
He will be my Guide, hold me closely to His side.
With love and strength for each new day,
He will make a way. He will make a way.

Through a roadway in the wilderness, He leads me.
Rivers in the desert will I see.
Heaven and earth will change, but His Word will still
    remain.
He will do something new - TODAY!"

God will make a way where there seems to be no way.
He works in ways we cannot see. He will make a way for
    me.
He will be my Guide, hold me closely to His side.
With love and strength for each new day,
He will make a way. He will make a way.

Don Moen

After campmeeting, Gloria went home and taught the song to her daughter, Nelita, who also loves music. They both loved it and sang it often together. One morning as they drove to school, they were singing the song, but there was one line neither could remember.

Arriving at the school, Nelita jumped out of the car, and ran to her first class, but this was not to be the usual day at school. She saw again that day that God answers prayer, and there's power in a song.

She wrote her experience for a Young Writer's Contest at her school. Let's let her tell the story:

> *"God will make a way, where there seems to be no way*
> *He works in ways we cannot see; He will make a*
> *   way for me.*
> *He will be my Guide, Hold me closely to His side.*
> *La da da dum, La da da dum,*
> *He will make a way, He will make a way.*

Mom and I were happily singing this song as she drove me to school. Although we didn't know one of the lines, we were content for the moment to replace the missing words with "la la la's." Upon arriving at school, I grabbed my books and jumped out of the car, mouthing the words, "I love you, Mom," as she drove away. Walking to the entrance, I continued to hum the song that had been a source of encouragement and strength to me as I tried to keep up with the onslaught of assignments from relentless teachers.

Later that morning, I bumped into Addie, who said, "Did you hear about Lenny?"

"Who?" I asked, puzzled.

"Hurricane Lenny. It is supposed to be coming our way tomorrow. The school is canceling the rest of today's classes."

"Cool!" I was thrilled. Tuesdays are especially grueling for me and I was glad to be going home early.

Back at home, I felt quite confident that Lenny was

nothing to lose sleep over, although weather reports described the storm as one of the weirdest in over a hundred years. Nevertheless, we Virgin Islanders prepared and waited for the mysterious guest. The only difference between preparing for a hurricane and preparing for a flesh-and-blood visitor, is the awareness that the hurricane guest will be a dangerous mix of vicious winds, pelting rain, and deafening thunder.

By Wednesday, November 17, 1999, I was feeling less stoic about the weather. Lenny had been upgraded to a potentially dangerous storm, and he was heading straight for St. Croix!

Mom and I spoke to Dad, a minister who was away on church business. I detected an undertone of anxiety in his voice as he cautioned us to be careful and assured us that he would be praying. By the time we hung up, the meteorologist announced that Lenny had strengthened to a category four hurricane, one category away from being the most devastating. Electricity was cut off for safety reasons, and we were now left in darkness, waiting for this disastrous storm to play out its performance on the stage of our lives. The eerie howling of the wind signaled the storm's ominous approach.

By around 3:00 PM, I attempted to keep my mind off the disturbing situation. Sitting at the piano, I attacked Chopin's "Military Polonaise." I was enjoying this diversion, when suddenly—it happened! There was a deafening CRASH in the dining room followed by a blinding flash of lightning.

"What was that?" I asked, making a bootless attempt to remain calm. However, I knew what had happened. Mom and I jumped up, and from the living room we peered into the dining room, afraid of what we might see. A rafter from the roof had crashed onto a dining chair. Half of the roof over the dining room had been viciously ripped away!

I froze. A million thoughts chased themselves through my mind: *"Why us? What are we gonna do now? This wasn't supposed to happen. I thought You'd protect us from this, Lord! This wasn't supposed to happen! What if the roof flies away? This wasn't supposed to happen! This was NOT supposed to happen!"*

"Hurry! Let's run to your room!" My mom's urgent command jolted me back to reality and we dashed through the dining room which was fast becoming flooded.

Let me add here, that our dining room houses well over a thousand books—our treasures. What would become of them? How painful to think that those books could be ruined! We turned our backs on the pitiful sight and headed for my cozy bedroom.

The sound of shrieking wind, convulsing trees, and pelting rain struck terror to my heart. I wanted to just sit on my bed and cry and feel sorry for myself; but Mom was being incredibly brave and strong. Why shouldn't I be? I could always cry after it was all over, but for now I had to concentrate on getting through the night.

Hours later, we heard Eileen, our neighbor, outside. There had been a slight lull and she had come to get us. We grabbed our emergency bag and bravely hurried through the storm to her house.

Hours of unabated weather plunged me deeper into despair. We suspected that few other families suffered such damage. Why us? God knew that Daddy was a missionary who had dedicated his life to the work of the church. Why did *our* family have to be the one to suffer?

We finally got Daddy on the phone. When we related the tragedy, I sensed the desperation in his voice as he repeatedly murmured, "Oh no, Oh no." I'll be home on the first available flight," he promised. My heart ached for him. This would be a terrible night for Daddy too.

That Wednesday night, each drop of rain pierced my heart as I imagined our home flooding. For comfort, I clung to my mother who lay beside me.

"Nel, wake up, Love," Mom whispered. It was morning. The hurricane had moved on, but I could still hear the moaning wind and gentle drizzle outside. I splashed cool water on my cheeks and brushed my teeth.

Softly, I said, "Mom, why isn't God strengthening me?" A lump had formed in my throat and I fought back the tears."

Back in the bed, Mom pulled me close, stroked my hair and whispered, "Let's ask God for His strength." And so, we unburdened our heavy hearts and spoke to a Father Who understood.

All the while, soothing religious songs floated from our faithful battery-operated radio. As soon as Mom said, "Amen," we heard it. A clear, tenor voice sang: *"God will make a way when there seems to be no way. ..."*

We couldn't believe it. We had never even heard that song on the radio until now. As I listened, tears spilled, hot and unrestrained, down my cheeks. My bitterness and pain melted as I absorbed this sign God sent just for me. He knew that I needed to hear those words that day. I felt God holding me and saying, "It's okay. Everything is going to be all right."

"Thank You," I whispered, ensconcing myself in His divine arms. I closed my eyes and got more rest out of the next two hours than I had had all night.

We returned home and bravely assessed the damage. It was not as bad as it could have been. As we cleaned up the mess (and marveled at how every book on the shelves in the dining room was *dry!*) I'm sure you can guess what we sang. This time, though, we were able to sing the missing words:

"With love and strength for each new day,
He will make a way. He will make a way."

Has your life been changed by singing God's music? David Ring, the successful evangelist, tells of a time when his life fell apart.

He was fourteen, when, at 5:30 one morning, the overhead light in his room came on. As he rubbed his eyes and tried to wake up, he saw his sister and brother-in-law standing in the doorway. They spoke three words that changed his life forever.

"She is gone," is all they said, and all they needed to say. His mother had been slowly losing the battle with cancer. They knew this was coming, but the blow was hard. David says, "My Mama was the only person in the world who really understood me. My Mama was the only one who cared. She accepted me, no matter what, and every day she told me that she loved me. Now she was gone."

All the way during the 5-hour drive to Jonesboro, Arkansas, his face was pressed up against the car window. Tears were streaming down his cheeks as he heard those words again and again—she is gone—she is gone—she is gone. Growing up with cerebral palsy had been difficult. There were cruel memories and sad times, but his Mama had always been there for him. But now she was gone.

After the funeral, they came back to Missouri to pick up their lives and return to some sense of "normal."

Each day after school, he returned to his sister's home. He was becoming difficult to live with—rebellious, but his sister wouldn't give up on him.

Each evening after dinner, his sister and brother-in-law would clear the table and clean up the kitchen. David would go into the living room and sit down beside the stereo. His favorite records were the gospel songs—songs by the "Happy Goodmans," the Speer Family, and others. At first, as he sat and listened, it was a time of grief and mourning for his mother. He listened to the words, but he was thinking about his Mama, and missing her warm arms around him.

Tears flooded his face as he asked the question, "Why, God?—Why did you take my Mama? Why did you take my Daddy? Why was I born with cerebral palsy? Why?"

But the words and melodies were reaching his heart with healing. He thought about the words, and he even started to sing along with the musicians. Something was happening in his soul. He said, "God came into that room, and pulled up a chair beside me in the Person of the Holy Spirit.

And God said, 'Keep singin,' boy, I like it.' God started to hum along with me. And God was massaging my heart."

Some time later, he went back to church with his sister —"just this once," and gave his heart to Christ. God was working. Things changed for David. Before this, he had no friends. Now he was Vice President of his class, and voted the "Most Popular" in school.

The amazing thing is that God can take the most devastating experiences and turn them into a blessing, the most painful experience becomes, "oil on your head." The very thing that may seem like the greatest hindrance can actually become a source of power, peace, and freedom. God can take the broken pieces and make something that is better than new.

Some medications contain ingredients that are harmful, but when they are mixed together in just the right proportions, and used for a specific need, they can actually be beneficial. God does that in our lives, as we praise Him, and are grateful, in the middle of our circumstances, for Who He is, and for what He can accomplish.

As we turn to Him in faith, singing our songs of trust and hope, He can change the circumstances and the way we relate to our "hopeless" situation.

Sing. Teach your children to sing. There is power in a song.

Contact David Ring Ministries
PO Box 682 286
Franklin, Tennessee 37068
615-771-9600
(For his book - *JUST AS I AM*, for videos, and other inspirational materials.)

Personal Applications by Noelene

Parenting at "Midnight"

Parents, particularly parents of teens, often view themselves negatively. Some parents cannot sing; some know nothing about child psychology or delivering a speech. Yet studies show us that parents have more influence in their child's life than anyone else. When teens were asked who influenced them most in their life, the vast majority responded, parents. Lined up against teachers, pastors, movie stars and politicians, parents win hands down! Why? Because of who they are—parents. The child has bonded to them. The attachment is strong and for life.

So parent, take heart. Make today a new beginning. Try one of the following activities with your kids. And in the coming months and years, try other activities. Come back to activities that work well with your family.

1. ***Parent talk.*** Speak to your child alone. Tell her that you love her, not because of the good deeds that she does, but for herself. Remind her of all the little things that make her special to you. Ask forgiveness for not being a perfect parent.

2. ***Love prayers.*** Pray together with your child that God will help your love grow so that whatever happens your child will never forget that he is loved.

3. ***Process your worries.*** Sit down as a family. Ask each person to think for a moment about their day then be prepared to tell what their number one worry is. Is it money, family, relationships with friends, problems connected with work, or fear of failure? Parents can go first and model honesty and vulnerability. But don't tell details that the kids don't need to know. Challenge everyone to give all their worries to Jesus and leave them

there. Promise each other not to talk outside the family about what was shared. Then kneel in a family circle, each praying for the concerns mentioned by the person to their left. Finally, sing a song of praise for Jesus who understands all our concerns.

4. **Family sing.** One night, turn off the TV and sing together your favorite hymns. Tell what makes that hymn special to you.

5. **Learn a song.** Choose one song to sing every day until the family has learned it by heart. Get enough copies of gospel songbooks for everyone to look on. Choose the book from a catalog of Adventist books.

6. **Start a family listening library.** Choose tapes/CDs of sacred music that are appropriate for your family. Encourage the whole family to contribute to a fund to purchase the tapes one at a time. Allow family members to choose music that is meaningful to them.

7. **Listening time.** Play uplifting music first thing in the morning and when the children are going to sleep. If you play an instrument, play that while the children are going to sleep. Years later they will remember the uplifting melodies that they heard you play.

8. **Signature tunes.** Encourage each person in the family to choose their own favorite hymn, a song that is important to them. Play and sing each person's hymn, memorizing the words. Pray the words of that hymn with the child at bedtime, highlighting phrases and sentiments that can be theirs to live by.

9. **Songs to share.** A memorable Internet story that is making the rounds, tells of a little boy who sang

"You are my Sunshine" to his new brother before he was born. When the baby was born prematurely, the big brother was distraught because the baby had to remain in an incubator instead of coming home with his mother, and because the hospital would not allow him to visit the baby. The premie was fighting for his life, but losing the battle when the mother sneaked the big brother into the nursery. In his joy, the older child began singing "You are my sunshine." That was a turning point for the little one. He began to improve. The family believes the improvement came because of the brother's song. As a family, identify a song that might be helpful to cheer everyone. Sing it often, especially when someone is feeling down.

10. **Gift list.** Give the gift of music. Purchase cheery Christian music as gifts for family and friends at Christmas, birthdays, or at someone else's midnight. Be ready as a family to tell your story and share the gift of your song when asked. Offer to sing for those who visit you at home and for those whom you visit. If you aren't singers, tell people that your talent is not in music and explain why you sing anyway. Give God all the glory because He is the one who likes your song, especially at midnight.

Scriptures for Midnight

"Therefore confess your sins to each other and pray for each other so that you may be healed. The prayer of a righteous man is powerful and effective" (James 5:16).

"But he was wounded for our transgressions, he was bruised for our iniquities: the chastisement of our peace was upon him; and with his stripes we are healed" (Isa. 53:5).

"If you are insulted because of the name of Christ, you are blessed, for the Spirit of glory and of God rests on you. If you suffer as a Christian, do not be ashamed, but praise God that you bear that name" (1 Pet. 4:15, 16).

"You will go out in joy and be led forth in peace; the mountains and hills will burst into song before you, and all the trees of the field will clap their hands" (Isa. 55:12).

"Those who sow in tears will reap with songs of joy. He who goes out weeping, carrying seed to sow, will return with songs of joy, carrying sheaves with him" (Ps. 126:5-6).

"The ransomed of the Lord will return. They will enter Zion with singing; everlasting joy will crown their heads. Gladness and joy will overtake them, and sorrow and sighing will flee away" (Isa. 55:11).

(Verses from NIV)

Chapter 2

The Everydays—
Capturing the golden moments

A speaker at a Christian Men's Conference recently provided an unforgettable experience. He had placed large traps at random places across the floor of the stage and around the podium where he stood. There were traps for bears, cougars, and for various other large animals.

Each one was carefully set, and placed so that there was little space left on the floor. In explaining his illustration, he drew parallels between these traps and something in a child or teenagers life—temptations, deceptions of the enemy to snare and destroy our children. He described the peer pressure, destructive habits, such as tobacco, drugs, wrong friends, wrong entertainment. Each trap represented something real, something tempting and attractive to a child or teen. Just as each trap would be set with food that the animal would want, each trap in a young person's life may look very tempting.

Steve, a teenager whom the speaker had asked to help with the demonstration, stood on the opposite side of the platform, waiting for his next instructions. As the speaker described the dangers in the world, traps for our children and youth, he didn't have to exaggerate, every adult knew the reality of the effects of the media, friends, and bad choices. Choices early in life affect the entire life.

The speaker then asked Steve to walk across the platform and join him at the front.

"Are you ready?" asked the man at the microphone. Steve hesitantly nodded. Then, just to make the demonstration a little more interesting, Steve was asked to take his shoes off. He thought about it a moment, and then slipped his shoes off.

The speaker next did something that made the audience gasp.

"Now, we need to make the situation as close to the "real world," as possible, so we're going to blindfold Steve. Our kids can't see the traps in their world. They don't recognize the real situation for what it is. The devil has disguised each one well." So someone came and tied a large black blindfold over Steve's eyes.

Discomfort rippled through the audience. How could he expect this kid to walk—in his stocking feet—blindfolded, across that crowded floor?

Then the speaker said, "All right, Steve, start walking!"

"STEVE, STOP! This is Dad!" Another voice immediately shouted. Steve's father was watching as the speaker was preparing each part, and at this point, he walked carefully across the platform until he stood directly in front of his blindfolded teenager. Placing Steve's hands on his own shoulders, he guided Steve slowly and deliberately across the platform until they were at the other side. And thousands of Christian men stood and cheered, with tears streaming down their faces as they saw father and son together walking to safety.

Every young person needs someone to walk in front, someone who cares, someone they can trust, someone who has experience with God, knowledge, and will take the time. It takes time to be there, to listen, to help a young mind make discoveries and right choices.

Children spell love T I M E. Parents, grandparents, aunts, uncles, and friends soon discover that there are golden moments that are priceless, and these moments can be found anywhere. The very best may be at the beginning and end of the day. Parents have precious opportunities in the morning to wrap arms of love around their children, to help them be prepared for what lies ahead, and at the end of the day, to listen, and to pray.

Kathleen, a mother of four, early every morning, went to each child's room. Bill, Denny, Nancy, and Patricia always knew that their "wake-up" would be hugs and kisses from their mother. This may have seemed like a ritual at the time, but it was a vital link to that mother's heart, and they loved it. She told them they were special. She laughed at their funny little jokes. They knew she would always be there for them.

Denny had a malignant tumor that shortened his life, but the other three are now adults. They grew up in a warm, happy environment blessed by loving parents who took just a few minutes every day to say "I love you. You're so special."

If our children are "wrapped around our hearts" they know they have the security of unconditional love.

The most valuable thing we can give them is to teach them to trust in their heavenly Father and Friend. How do you teach a child to pray? How do you guide young hearts and instill values that will last for eternity?

There are eternal realities that you hold dear, that have been your beacon, guiding your decisions through life, and now—to instill this excitement, this vision, into your children! What an honor, responsibility and privilege!

Someone has said our children are like wet cement, and God is ready to use your hands, your mind, your heart as these characters are formed. His angels "rejoice that they can use our lips," so you have been promised the highest help possible.

But don't wait for some "perfect opportunity" for your child to ask just the "right" question, and you'll *know* they're ready. There are golden moments everywhere if you look for them. Ask the Holy Spirit to open your mind, and the mind and curiosity of your child.

Our prayers for our children and grandchildren are powerful to prepare the way. My friend, Ginny Allen, has two granddaughters who have both been prayed for since before they were born. Each one has had the encouragement and special influence of very specific prayers from her grandmother.

Ginny said, "I have prayed daily that Ashley will want to obey God, to know Him, and to love Him." These prayers are being answered in specific ways to let Ginny and Ashley know that God hears.

Recently I heard a father tell how he had been crushed by hearing one of his children as she told a friend, "I *never* get to see Daddy!" He knew it was true, and he asked God to help him change it before it was too late. He vowed that he would make changes in his schedule to give his children the gift of himself—the gift of time. He wanted desperately to change the picture, and he did.

One of the daily changes was to give each child 15-30 minutes each night before they went to sleep. His children were thrilled to have him lie beside them on their beds and just to "listen" to their thoughts and the ups and downs of their day. This was when they prayed together and memorized Scripture.

Now, no matter what pressures are in his schedule, when he is home, they know that they can look forward to these times at night with Dad. It has changed their lives. It has changed the way they feel about their Daddy, and the way they feel about their Heavenly Father. It has also changed their home, their lives at school, and their plans for the future.

It may seem like such a little thing, but a prayer habit with parents and kids can make a magnificent difference. It gives God opportunities to mold and shape and change lives—for parents as well as children.

These quiet times together, however accomplished, provide the environment—while the day's memories are still fresh—to reflect, to learn, and to grow. Maybe there has been something wonderful that needs to be enjoyed together.

One of the most encouraging things a youngster can hear is "I'm so proud of you! You did just the right thing!" These are the happy, golden moments. They naturally lead to thankfulness to our Father in heaven Who provides for His children in greater ways than we can ask.

Children can learn while very young that Jesus loves them and is with them. They learn to be thankful, not only to their parents, but to God, for the big things and for the little things that are so important to them.

My niece Teri and her husband Tedd are in North Dakota, where Tedd is the Gymnastics Coach at Dakota Adventist Academy. Tedd and I were talking about their children recently on the phone. I said, "Tedd, how did you and Teri teach Jessica (10) and Jordan (7) to pray?"

He said, "It's a little like developing their muscular skills. They crawl, stand, learn to balance, then walk, and finally they're running. It's like that as our children learn to pray, they begin to realize that God loves them. Because they had no understanding or experience in 'talking to someone they can't see' they have to imitate us. For them, it starts with the basic skills of prayer and builds as they grow. They started by covering their eyes to thank Jesus for their food. Then they said, 'Dear Jesus, thank you for my food, Amen'. Now, it's fascinating to see their growth and faith."

Jordy, at 6, was very aware of the tornadoes that had swept through parts of North Dakota, and was afraid of something that powerful and destructive. Children at that age may have some unique fears. They may be afraid of the dark, afraid of bad dreams, or of something that may even seem irrational to an adult.

Their little world has not given them the vantage point yet, the frame of reference, and they are still processing all the incoming information. Jordan had seen the news on TV that had shown homes and whole communities destroyed. This had even touched some areas close to where they live, and his prayers were for protection, asking Jesus to keep him and his family safe from the tornadoes.

I talked to Jordan about this on the phone one evening. I can always count on his creativity, his quick little mind. After we talked about the usual things, like— "When are you coming to see me?" I asked him about talking to Jesus.

"Jordan, why do you like to talk to Jesus?" I asked him.

"Because He's STRONG!" He answered. He knew that God could take care of the tornadoes or anything else. Our great God even takes takes negative or scary things in a child's life to help him learn spiritual truths.

"Does Jesus love you, Jordan?" I asked.

"YES!" was his emphatic reply. We talked about some of the ways that Jesus shows Jordan that He loves him. Jordan just believes—which must bring joy to the heart of God.

His sister, Jessica's prayers reflect her own personality and her developing understanding of Jesus. Jessica thanks Jesus for specific things, and then she often prays for everyone on their street—all 12 homes, and everyone in each house. Sometimes her prayers seem a little prolonged, and may bring smiles to her parents, but she's just talking to Someone Who is listening and Who cares. She wants Him to know when she's concerned about her family or friends. At this young age, she's developing her "finer motor skills" of prayer, of intercession for others.

Tedd says that the finer skills of prayer have to include a deep trust and a vulnerability based on knowing and believing God. This is something children learn as they watch their parents. So much is caught, understood, and imitated.

"It's like basketball—maybe it's a little like shooting baskets," Tedd said. "It's like practicing without a backboard and a ring you can see. If you see it in your mind, and practice carefully, you "know" when you've made a basket, even if you can't see it with your eyes. And it's like that with prayer. You trust, even when you can't see, because you know from past experience He can be trusted. You know that what He has promised in His word is true, and you can keep on believing and thanking Him." That's how Tedd and Teri would describe the "fine motor skills of prayer"—trust, faith, being vulnerable with God, and knowing Him through His Word.

Components of Prayer

Jessica doesn't call her prayers **intercession**, but she's interceeding for others. When we unselfishly, on our knees, take others to God's throne, we are interceding on their behalf. Dick Eastman, who has written many wonderful books on prayer has called intercession, *love on its knees.* That's a good description—caring enough about others to take them to God in prayer.

My husband reminds me that intercession is truly one of the most valuable and most unselfish acts of the Christian. It takes time, thought, earnestness, a desire for God to work in the life of someone else. But you never get the credit for it, because it is just between you and God. When He answers, only God is praised. But the pray-er is rewarded too, and children understand at an early age that unselfishness, giving to others, has its own deep rewards. Praying for others brings double strength—these prayers are a help to the pray-er *and* those we pray for.

Jordy's prayers were for himself. This is another kind of prayer that our children need to learn to pray—for themselves. We call these prayers of **petition**. It means showing them where to get help for their very specific personal needs.

Begin simply for the very young child, and let it become a natural and growing experience as their needs change. By sharing how you pray for yourself, they can see that you depend on God and need Him too.

Then, even with the very young child, we can suggest specific favors they can ask of God. That Jesus will live inside and take away a bad temper. That Jesus will control her lips so she says only kind words. As Mom or Dad lead the way with genuine requests, kids soon catch on.

Another kind of prayer is **silent prayer & waiting.**
Children learn that they can ask God to make their
heart a quiet place. Quietness in His presence is a
treasure, and children and young people love it. Here
they can learn the value of silent prayer, and that
prayer is being with God. Silent prayer is a special gift
we can return to anytime because He is with us. His
angels are taking these silent prayers to God's throne
and He is there to listen and to answer. As we wait
quietly in His presence, He not only quiets the heart,
but enables you to surrender your soul to Him.

Using stories and texts from Scripture can open up
another adventure: **Scripture prayer.** As you read a
verse or two, what thoughts come to mind that you'd
like to discuss with God? Would you like to remind
Him of a promise, or just to thank Him for speaking to
you? For older children and young people, the triumphal entry in Matthew 21 opens a beautiful time of
prayer for individual, twos, or small groups in a
directed prayer time. (See appendix)

My friend, Kathi, is a warm, intelligent, and spiritually-
gifted mother. Her little son, Kevin, who struggles
with his temper, is the focus of her nearly constant
prayers. She sometimes puts little cards with special
promises around where he can see them. He can't
read, but he is very bright, and even at 3, has learned
to understand and remember each one. These were little flags to him, and reminders that the angels were
there to help him. This is actually a form of Scripture
praying, because the prayers claim promises tailor-
made to the needs.

Confession & Forgiveness—There's another important component of prayer—a time for reflection, of
admitting, of keeping short accounts with God.

At the end of the day children are often more relaxed
and ready to share something that happened during
the day, something that may have caused fear or hurt.

If there has been something to be settled, they learn while very young about forgiveness, of wiping the slate clean.

God disciplines His children, but never in anger—only in grief because of what our disobedience causes. Someone has said, "You never get the back of the hand" from God.

Michael Kelly Blanchard, in his Christian ballad, *"I Love You, I Do, You Bet"* tells of his mother, who instituted something in their family she called "chat." This meant that you had to tell it all, but there would only be forgiveness and the loving arms of God. The chorus of his ballad says:

> *"There is nothing so bad you can't confide in me, Love —*
> *No sorrow or lasting regret.*
> *Nothing so bad that you've tried to be free of,*
> *That I won't forgive and forget —*
> *Because I love you, I do.*
> *I love you, it's true.*
> *I love you, I do. You bet.*

He told of a time when he had stolen a little car from the "five and dime" store. He suffered in silence, ashamed of himself, but couldn't get it out, until his mother said it was time for a "chat." When he was finally able to confess what he'd done, she said she could almost hear the angels clap.

He has remembered that experience all his life. He learned that God loves, He forgives, and forgets. He learned that it is vital to confess, to admit to God and to appropriate others, and to receive peace, grace, and cleansing.

What a difference that made in his life, and it makes a difference in our lives too. This freeing confession prayer teaches us and our children something profound about the heart of God.

A friend of ours spoke harshly to his 10-year-old daughter, Beth, during dinner one evening. That night at bedtime he asked her forgiveness and prayed that Jesus would forgive him too, and help him to speak kindly.

After the prayer, Beth said, "Dad, I knew you were going to have to say that."

Teachers can help to complement the teaching of parents. They can reinforce and support a child's spiritual growth. I asked my daughter-in-law, Mimi, who teaches First Grade at the Ruth Murdoch Elementary School in Berrien Springs, Michigan, how she does this.

She said, "Mom, children in the first grade are so natural." They're genuine, no pretense. Their prayers are open, telling God exactly how they feel. They want to give Him the burdens of their little hearts. They see Jesus as their Friend, and they want to talk to Him. When they get older, they may get more self-conscious. They've heard adults pray and may think that their prayers aren't as "polished." But first-graders are uninhibited and just want to tell God how it is."

Singing—We may not realize that many hymns and little choruses are often words of Scripture and were written as prayers. Try singing these songs with your child, with or without your eyes closed, concentrating on the words, and singing them as praise, worship, or petition. My friend, Ginny Allen, likes to begin her worship time each morning by singing something to the Lord. This is one of her favorites:

> This is the day, this is the day that the Lord has made, that the Lord has made.
> I will rejoice, I will rejoice and be glad in it, and be glad in it.
> This is the day that the Lord has made. I will be glad and rejoice in it.
> This is the day, this is the day that the Lord has made.

Another happy song of faith for worship and prayer is this one:

In my life, Lord, be glorified, be glorified,
In my life, Lord, be glorified, today.

Adults and children love to sing Scripture songs. It is a beautiful way of putting these words into our minds, and etching them on the walls of our memories.

It's amazing how the words of a song will flow through your mind throughout the day. The melody helps you remember the words. Songs are important in heaven. There they sing a new song, and we are told to do that here. Try composing a new song for your prayer time. Help your child to form the words and melodies to a new song.

Thanksgiving prayers may be the easiest to teach because there are specific things to be thankful for—we can thank Him for creating the flowers, the birds, our food, and any special gift. Thanksgiving is different from praise. While prayers of praise are prayers of adoration for His power or His character, prayers of thanksgiving are specific prayers of gratitude for something God has done for you.

For many children, their first, simple prayers may be at mealtime, when they're still drinking from their "tippy" cup. With the help of Mom or Dad, they'll be able to start with "Dear Jesus, thank You for my food. Amen." Then the prayers will develop as they grasp the significance.

Personal Applications by Noelene

Looking for Golden Moments

God's golden moments are sometimes called teachable moments. Children become hushed and want to talk about God. A thoughtful gaze or a penetrating question will be your cue. Golden moments can happen at the close of a day, by the fire, around the dinner table, just before or after lights out, as well as at the conclusion of a story, game, or activity. Golden moments cannot be commanded or orchestrated. One never quite knows when they will come, but when they do, we need to stop what we have planned and make the best of our opportunity. Golden moments sometimes come when we abandon routine to do something special like playing hide-and-seek, flying kites, taking a long walk, or star gazing. Television can spark a golden moment, but more often than not it extinguishes them. Golden moments can be teachable moments that lead to prayer.

Expanding on Golden Moments. When you sense a golden moment at the close of a story, such as Zaccheus, help your little Zaccheus to see herself "up a tree." (Every story in the Bible, by the way, reminds us that we all are up a tree.) Ask: *What do you think God is trying to tell us? If you were in that story, which person do you think you would be? Which person would you rather be? Why? How does that make you feel about God? And to seal the moment: What would you like to tell God now?*

Family Worship Ideas

Activities at family worship time can generate golden moments. Try some or all of the following with the family or with a child individually at bedtime. Look for the golden moment. Then let go of your agenda and let the Lord lead.

1. **Family Pow! Wow!** Sit cross legged on the bed or on the floor. If you have an Indian necklace or moccasins, wear them. Say: *Let's have a pow! wow! First, the pow! What was the worst thing that happened today?* Pause as long as it takes for someone to speak up. If at first nobody responds, tell your *pow!* Then wait. After the kids talk, ask them how they feel about what happened to them; encourage them to talk to Jesus about it. If the *pow!* was something they did wrong, encourage them to say they're sorry, maybe even calling the person concerned to apologize. Then for a booster, ask the kids to tell their *wow!* Ask: What was the best thing that happened today? Praise God for the *wow!s.* Show children that all the praise and glory belong to God.

2. **Variation on the Pow! Wow!** Call a pow! wow! any time that something significant grabs your family's attention. For the pow!: ask family members to talk about what troubles them about what happened. For the wow!: ask them what pleased them about the incident or what good they think may come from it.

3. **Meal Time Conversations.** Begin a family routine of sitting down to eat meals together. Table conversation can generate golden moments. A pow! wow! can begin unannounced around the table.

4. **Family Activities.** Recently, a grown man stood weeping beside his father's casket. "You can't know how much I loved that man," he whispered to his pastor. "There were three of us boys and we each had one night a week where we could name what we wanted to do and Dad went along and did it with us. He must have been tired after a day of

work, but he never mentioned it. We went bike riding and hiking; we played ball. Nothing was too much bother." Doing something together can spark a golden moment as well as great memories.

5. ***Family Prayers.*** From the earliest years, teach children to kneel and pray to start the day. Try to be at their bedside when they wake up; make prayer the bright, cheery thing to do. Pray again as a family in the evening and then pray with each child separately when you say goodnight. Let them hear you each night thank God that you are their parent. Assure them of your love and their acceptance with God.

6. ***Family Trust Walk.*** Blindfold one child while you or the rest of the family rearrange chairs, cushions, etc. to create a maze. (Or have the child wait while you rearrange the furniture.) Spin the child around several times and then ask the child to cross the room to a specific point you name (the door, the piano, etc.). Explain that the object is to reach the other side without touching anything. Even if they brush a piece of furniture they are out and must start over or give someone else a turn. To raise the excitement level for older children, time them. When the child realizes that she cannot do it alone, offer to guide her. Take her hand or tell her how many steps to take, when to change direction, and when to stop. Celebrate each step with affirmation. Read John 10:3-5 and ask: *How might a trust walk help us understand what Jesus is saying in these verses?* (God's children listen to God and to parents/teachers.)

Repeat performance: Change the course a little each time they attempt the walk. When the activity gets to be ho-hum, have other voices, possibly recorded, shouting conflicting directions so the child must concentrate on your voice. Ask: *What does this activity teach you about living God's way?* (You can't do it alone; you need to listen to Jesus.)

7. ***The Song of the King.*** Read together *The Song of the King*, an illustrated book by Max Lucado (Crossway Books, available at Christian book stores and Amazon.com). Discuss the following with older children: Who do you know who is like the king in this story? (God.) Who do you know who is like the prince? (Jesus) If you were a knight, who would you choose to go with you on a long journey? (The prince, Jesus) Read John 10:3-5. What might this story be telling you about you and Jesus? (Take their responses seriously. The responses will vary according to the age of the child.)

8. ***Celebrating success.*** Look for excuses to celebrate family successes. Define success as somebody trying real hard, whether the results are perfect or not. Success is also when others offer compliments about your family or a family member. Success can be celebrated when a child has made improvement or put forth super effort. Celebrations can be simple commendation, a pat on the back, high fives, or some sort of treat. Whatever, always make God a part of the celebration. Give thanks to God for His hand in it: for giving health, strength, a clear mind, determination, and faithfulness. Or for helping the child and her talents to grow. Help children to recognize success as being a gift of God's grace.

Ages and stages of prayer

A young mother recently asked how to pray with little children. Prayer has a place in a child's entire life. Children grow in prayer just as in any other phase of their lives. Nobody can set a timetable for prayer; individual children grow in their own way in their own time. The following is a broad sketch of what to do and what to look for at different ages and stages.

Prenatal. Pray out loud every evening and morning. If possible, both father and mother can pray. Edwina Neely, a pastor's wife in Maryland, tells of her husband reading "Child Guidance" aloud and praying every evening while they awaited their youngest daughter's birth. After delivery, the baby began to cry, but when Bill Neely spoke, the child immediately quieted. She recognized her father's voice.

Newborn. Continue family devotions, bringing the baby into the circle especially when praying. Cuddle him close. Pray or sing a prayer at the crib when putting the child down at night. You can use a traditional prayer or make up your own.

Now I Lay Me Down (Tune: *"Jesus Loves Me"*)

> *Now I lay me down to sleep*
> *I pray You, Lord, my soul to keep.*
> *If I should die before I wake,*
> *I pray You, Lord, my soul to take.*
> —*Traditional*

Gentle Jesus Meek and Mild (Tune: *"Twinkle, Twinkle, Little Star"*)

> *Gentle Jesus meek and mild,*
> *Look upon a little child.*
> *Pity my simplicity*
> *And suffer me to come to Thee.*
> *Gentle Jesus meek and mild,*
> *Look upon a little child. Amen*   —*Traditional*

Come Close, Dear Jesus (Tune: *"Rock-a-bye Baby"*)

> *Come close, Dear Jesus,*
> *Be here to stay.*
> *Watch over Baby;*
> *Bless her we pray.*
> *All through the darkness*

May she sleep tight.
Keep our sweet baby
Till morning light

        —Noelene Johnsson

Infant. As the child begins to take solid food from a spoon, put his hands gently together, brush your fingers lightly over his eyes and pray a one sentence prayer.

    "Dear Jesus, thank you for the food. Amen."

Infants will not stay in an attitude of prayer for long. So if necessary, pray a shorter prayer.

    "Thank You, Jesus, Amen"

Make a big thing of "Amen," hugging each other after it is said. Soon the little one will say "Amen" before you.

Toddler. Continue to embrace the child as you pray in family worship. (Family worship may be only you and the child.) Point out pictures of Jesus in books. Whisper His name. Say: "Let's talk to Jesus." Soon the child will say "Dear Jesus" and "Amen" unaided. If a family prayer continues beyond the child's attention span, allow him to drop out of the prayer.

Preschool. Prayer will grow parallel to the child's speaking skills and stage of thinking. As the 3-year-old learns to name objects, she will say a simple prayer after you and then ask God to bless people whom she can name. For instance:

Dear Jesus (*Dear Jesus*),
I love you (*I love you*).
God, bless Mommy (*God bless Mommy*)
And Daddy (*And daddy and ... ad infinitum*)
Amen.

Later when the God bless part is mastered, add the

thank you's:

Thank you for the sunshine (*Thank you for the
    sunshine*).
Thank you for flowers (*Thank you for flowers ...
    ad infinitum*).
Amen.

Gradually the child will say thank you for things of
her choosing.

Lower elementary. Children can pray prayers of
praise, intercession, confession, and petition with the
help of an adult. They do so in a natural conversation
style. But they may pray just one kind of prayer at a
time. As children learn their memory verses you can
encourage them to pray about some aspect of the
verse. Children of this age find it easy to memorize.
You might write a more grown-up prayer for them to
learn. Encourage them to add their own thanks and
requests for other people. Children who have memorized a grown-up prayer will never be stuck for what
to say if asked to pray at church.

Upper Elementary. If you always pray the above ele-
ments in the same order and beginning with the same
words, kids may remember to include them all sooner.
Some acronyms can be used to cue the memory. For
instance: ACTS: Adoration, confession, thanksgiving,
supplication. Or PART: praise, admit (confession),
request, thank.

Chapter 3

Sharing Stories

Doesn't everybody love a story? And stories are wonderful vehicles to make impressions on the heart. They provide the "spoonful of sugar" to allow you to relive, through someone else's experience, what it felt like, what it means, and Who we can talk to about it. Stories help us relate to life's difficult situations with a clarity that may not be available without just the right experience to shed the necessary light.

Max Lucado, a master of story-telling, has written some extraordinary books for children that can be an exciting launch pad for parents and teachers to use in developing spiritual experiences in the lives of their children.

In his book, "*Children of the King*," he tells about five orphans who were adopted by a king. They were told, by adults, that kings like to be impressed, so they must give him gifts. Now it happens that these adults who were advising the children didn't really know the king.

So the children set about the work of preparing their gifts. All except for one little girl who had no talent, but "who had a good heart." Her only gift was to help others. She listened to travelers and others at the city gate. Her siblings were carving, practicing music, painting, or studying, all as gifts to their new father, the king. She had no gift except her heart for others. She met the people of the village as they returned from their travels, and asked about their trip, their families, their lives. She groomed their horses and gave them a drink while the travelers rested.

When the king came for his children, he came in the disguise of a traveler. She met him and listened as he spoke. She brushed his horse as he slept. When he returned, he told her that those he came to see were all too busy for him.

One was carving a beautiful gift of soft and precious wood. He had no time for the traveler. One was singing and the applause of her listeners was so loud that she couldn't hear the voice of the king. Another was so absorbed in the sunset she was painting that she didn't even see him waiting to talk with her.

One brother had gone away, now a great scholar, attending a famous school. No one was willing to take the time for the king—except the little one whose only gift for him was time to talk. With this parable, Lucado gives the opening for reflective dialogue with your child. God is so eager for His children to spend time with Him—time in His Word, time in His presence, time appreciating Him and listening to His voice. This is what changes us.

Can children be taught that listening in prayer is important? Listening, as prayer, is sometimes over-looked. In our hurry, we don't often pause to listen to God's voice through His Word, and through the voices in nature, or as He speaks to our hearts by His Holy Spirit. To listen is to be open to His words of instruc-tion and guidance, which are always in agreement with His Word in Scripture. Listening is being pliable to the Holy Spirit and being yielded to His direction in our lives.

In the "*Song of the King*" Lucado tells about three famous knights who all were vying for the hand of the princess. The King promised that the young man who was able to find his way to the castle by way of the

Hemlock Forest would be the winner. All three were intimidated by the Hemlock Forest, even though they were brave and strong men. This forest was the home of the Hopenots, and everyone had heard stories of what happened to those venturing into the darkness of the home of the Hopenots.

The knights were told that in order to find their way safely through the forest, they must listen to the song of the king. He would play a golden flute three times each day, and this would provide the guidance and direction they would need. They were each allowed to take one traveling companion. So they set out.

One of the men, Alon, was known for his quickness. He was fast, and was famous for his escapes. His victories in the past were often due to his ability to outrun and outmaneuver others. Another of the knights, Carlisle, was known for his great strength. He could battle with power. Cassidon was known for his quick mind, his alertness. The prince explained that there were only two flutes, his own, and the king's.

The people in the village at the castle were waiting day after day, anxious for the word of the men traveling through the forest. Finally one day, two men, on foot, were seen coming out of the forest toward the castle. The king gave instructions to give them medical help and to prepare for the banquet to receive them.

As everyone assembled for the big event, they were curious to see who would be the winner—would it be the man of great strength? Many were sure he was the only one who could make it through the forest. Would it be Alon, who could be so swift? Once again, the king played the flute, and again everyone stopped to listen. And as he played, Cassidon and his companion came into the king's presence.

Everyone had questions. How were the Hopenots?

How did they get through the Hemlock Forest? Cassidon explained that the Hopenots were fearsome, and it was extremely difficult. They had stolen Cassidon's horses, and had made travel hard, but the worst part was that they were imitators. When Cassidon tried to listen for the king's flute, the Hopenots played distracting songs on their own flutes.

The obvious question came. How did Cassidon know the king's song?

He had chosen the right companion—the prince who alone knew the king's song. When Cassidon was confused by the distractions of the Hopenots and their songs, he listened to the prince's golden flute, right beside him, playing the king's song.

Appealing stories, calling for thoughtful questions, create wonderful times to listen to our children—to hear their thoughts about the story and about life. If we just read the story, and leave them, turn out the light and say "Good Night," we have missed a wonderful, teachable moment. Children are alert and want to grasp all that there is in a story. Their creative minds will soak it in like a sponge, and take these powerful truths to their hearts.

Who doesn't enjoy a good Christmas story? But there are stories that come to us at Christmas time with so many character-building truths, we would do well to remember them all year. Here's one that came to me by e-mail, and is full of with lessons to remember and to put into practice:

Bobby was getting cold sitting out in his back yard in the snow. Bobby didn't wear boots; he didn't like them, and anyway, he didn't own any. The thin sneakers he wore had a few holes in them and they were doing a poor job of keeping out the cold.

Bobby had been in his back yard for about an hour

already. And, try as he might, he could not come up with an idea for his mother's Christmas gift. He shook his head as he thought, "This is useless, even if I do come up with an idea, I don't have any money to spend."

Ever since his father had died three years ago, the family of five had struggled. It wasn't because his mother didn't care, or try, there just never seemed to be enough. She worked nights at the hospital, but the small wage that she was earning could only be stretched so far. What the family lacked in money and materials things, they more than made up for in love and family unity.

Bobby had two older sisters and one sister younger. The older ones ran the household in their mother's absence. All three of his sisters had already made beautiful gifts for their mother. Somehow it just wasn't fair. Here it was Christmas Eve already, and he had nothing.

Wiping a tear from his eye, Bobby kicked the snow and started to walk down the street where the shops and stores were. It wasn't easy being six without a father, especially when he needed a man to talk to.

Bobby walked from shop to shop, looking into each decorated window. Everything seemed so beautiful and so out of reach. It was starting to get dark and Bobby reluctantly turned to walk home when suddenly his eyes caught the glimmer of the setting sun's rays reflecting off something along the curb. He reached down and discovered a shiny dime. Never before has anyone felt so wealthy as Bobby felt at that moment. As he held his new-found treasure, a warmth spread throughout his entire body and he walked into the first store he saw.

His excitement quickly turned cold when the salesperson told him that he couldn't buy anything with only a dime. He saw a flower shop and went inside to wait in line. When the shop owner asked if he could help him, Bobby presented the dime and asked if he could buy one flower for his mother's Christmas gift.

The shop owner looked at Bobby and his ten-cent offering. Then he put his hand on Bobby's shoulder and said to him, "You just wait here and I'll see what I can do for you." As Bobby waited, he looked at the beautiful flowers and even though he was a boy, he could see why mothers and girls liked flowers so much.

The sound of the door closing as the last customer left, jolted Bobby back to reality. All alone in the shop, Bobby began to feel alone and afraid. Suddenly, the shop owner came out and moved to the counter. There, before Bobby's eyes, lay 12 long stemmed, red roses, with leaves of green and tiny white flowers all tied together with a big silver bow.

Bobby's heart sank as the owner picked them up and placed them gently into a long white box lined with green paper. "That'll be ten cents, young man," the shop owner said, reaching out his hand for the dime.

Slowly, Bobby moved his hand to give the man his dime. Could this be true? No one else would give him a thing for the dime! Sensing the boy's reluctance, the shop owner added, "I just happened to have some roses on sale for ten cents a dozen. Would you like them?"

This time, Bobby didn't hesitate, and when the man placed the long box into his hands, he knew it was true. Walking out the door, the owner was holding open for Bobby, he heard the shop keeper say, "Merry Christmas, son."

As he returned inside, the shop keeper's wife walked out. "Who were you talking to back there, and where are the roses you were fixing?" She asked.

Staring out the window, and blinking the tears from his own eyes, he replied, "A strange thing happened to me this morning. While I was setting up things to open the shop, I thought I heard a voice telling me to set aside a dozen of my best roses for a special gift. I wasn't sure at the time whether I had lost my mind or what, but I set them aside anyway.

Then, just a few minutes ago, a little boy came into the shop and wanted to buy a flower for his mother with one small dime. When I looked at him, I saw myself, many years ago. I, too, was a poor boy with nothing to buy my mother a Christmas gift. A bearded man, whom I had never met stopped me on the street and told me that he wanted to give me ten dollars."

"When I saw that little boy tonight, I knew Who that voice was, and I put together a dozen of my very best roses."

The shop owner and his wife hugged each other tightly, and as they stepped out into the bitter cold air, they somehow didn't feel cold at all.

Personal Applications by Noelene

Family Worship Ideas

In Old Testament times the patriarch Abraham, when he pitched camp, set up nearby an altar for family worship. We know the genealogies and stories from Adam were passed on orally. Abraham may possibly have passed them on to Isaac at the family altar. Even today nomadic tribes without a written language tell their history through stories around evening fires. The practice passes on a sense of family and of place in the world.

Telling our stories is still important because that is how we best pass on our faith. So, if you already have family prayers, why not expand that time, morning and evening, to include telling stories. Call it story time and see how well children will respond. In the morning families can focus on a Bible story. At night, tell your story.

If mornings are rushed so that your family feels there is not time for stories, try turning off the TV earlier at night for one month, or turn it off altogether. Retiring and rising half-hour earlier will offer a way for your young Cassidon's to hear the "King's song." Try some of the following worship ideas and enjoy the change family worship can make.

1. **Just do it.** If you are not accustomed to taking time for family worship, gather the family together and tell them the story *"The Song of the King,"* by Max Lucado. (You can order it from a Christian book store or from amazon.com. Explain that the best way to hear the King's song is to worship as a family every morning and and evening. Plan together for the changes in routine that may be needed. And then just do it. Starting tomorrow morning. Lest you fall back into the old habits,

give this part of your family life into God's hands. Ask Him to help you wake early and to make your first thoughts of Him. Families do not earn grace by having family worship, but worship time opens our hearts to grace that is already there.

2. **Morning worship.** Read all or part of a Bible story, such as the assigned children's lesson from church. One morning read it from the Bible. Study the daily study guide provided or ask children the following questions: *What is God trying to tell us in this story? What do you think this story tells us about God? About you?*

3. **Evening worship.** Talk about the day and pray. Take time to do an activity or tell a story. Often the children's lesson suggests an activity that you can do as a family. Or tell a story from your own life or from a character-building book. Watch for the golden moment and take time to ask the kids: *How do you feel about the story? What was (name of character in the story) feeling? What part do you think God played in this story?*

4. **Grace hunt.** Grace is free, it's from God, it's a gift. We have no part in it; God does it all. Grace is Jesus saving us, healing us, making us whole. It's God loving us unconditionally. So challenge the kids every Tuesday to look for grace in their Bible story and in their day. (Why do this Tuesday? Because "Tuesday's child is full of grace.")

5. **Grace clippers.** Look for "Tuesday's Child," an ongoing children's worship page in the weekly *Adventist Review.* Clip these and other grace stories and save them in a scrapbook. Grace stories are not real common, but they lift the spirits as no other type of story can.

6. **ABC names of Jesus.** Spend an interesting worship with older children every once in a while try-

ing to find a name of Jesus for each letter of the alphabet. Or just read aloud the list below. The apostles experienced the power of Jesus' name; they prayed with confidence: "Protect them by the power of Your name" (John 17:11).

Names of Jesus

A– Alpha (means first), All Powerful, Author of Salvation (Heb. 2:10)

B– Bread of God (John 6:33), Baby Jesus, Builder of everything (Heb. 3:4)

C– Creator, Christ, Commander of (God's) army (Josh. 5:13)

D– Dayspring (Luke 1:78, KJV), Deliverer (2 Sam 22:2)

E– Everlasting Father, Emmanuel (God with us)

F– Friend, Finisher of our faith, Fortress (2 Sam. 22:2)

G– God, Gate to the sheepfold, Good Shepherd

H– Hope of Israel, High Priest (Heb:3:1), Holy One of Israel

I– I am, Intercessor

J– Jesus, Joy, Judge

K– King of Kings

L– Life, Lilly of the Valley, Lord of Lords, Light of the world (John 1)

M– Morning star, Michael, Most High (Ps. 9), Master, Mighty God

N– The name above all names

O– Omego (last), One and only Son (John 3:16)

P– Prince of Peace, Priest Forever (Heb. 5:16), Pillar of cloud

R– Rose of Sharon, Rock (2 Sam. 22:2), Rabbi, Redeemer

S– Son, Savior, Solid Rock, Seat of Mercy, Shield (2 Sam. 22:3)

T– Truth, Teacher, True Vine, Temple Veil that was torn

V– Vine, Valiant Aid

W– Way, Water of Life, Word, Wonderful

Y– Yahweh

Z– Zion's King

7. **Pray the names of Jesus.** Ask: *What kind of a God do you feel like you need tonight?* A preschool child who has been bullied or put down might choose Comforter, Mighty God, or Commander of the army of the Lord (Josh.5:13). Or a sick child might prefer Great Doctor or Heavenly Physician. You can address God by that name as you pray, asking for the appropriate need (strength, protection, healing, etc.).

8. **Personalized text.** Seek the guidance of the Holy Spirit as you choose a text for each child. Tell the child: *This is your text today. Let's look it up and read it.* After discussing what God might be trying to say through the text, pray using the words of the text. Pray the same text every day until the child has memorized it.

Scripture to pray with children

We are told that "Prayer is heaven's ordained means of success in the conflict with sin and the development of Christian character." (Acts of the Apostles, 564) To make prayer especially meaningful, base a prayer on a Bible text, such as the child's personal text or their memory verse.

You will find, however, that the most effective scripture to pray with children is a passage or text that you find in your own devotions and share with the children or that they find themselves. Below are some passages that we found:

Texts for tough times

- *"Call upon me in the day of trouble; I will deliver you, and you will honor me." (Ps. 50:15)*

- *"For the eyes of the Lord range throughout the earth to strengthen those whose hearts are fully committed to him." (2 Chron. 16:9)*

- *"Those who are with us are more than those who are with them." (2 Kings 6:16)*

- *"If you follow my decrees and are careful to obey my commands . . . . five of you will chase a hundred, and a hundred of you will chase ten thousand, and your enemies will fall . . . before you." (Lev. 26:3, 8)*

Words of comfort

- *"Weeping may remain for a night, but rejoicing comes in the morning." (Ps. 30:5)*

- *"I was young and now I am old, yet I have never seen the righteous forsaken or their children begging bread." (Ps. 37:25)*

- "He will wipe every tear from their eyes. There will be no more pain, for the old order of things has passed away." (Rev. 21:4)

Good advice for pre adolescents

- "The fear of the Lord— that is wisdom, and to shun evil is understanding." (Job 28:28)

- "Walk before me in integrity of heart and uprightnees as David . . . did." (1 Kings 9:14)

- "I can of my own self do nothing." (John 5:30)

- "God, who reconciled us to himself through Christ ... gave us the ministry of reconciliation." (2 Cor. 5:18)

Assurance

- "The one who trusts in him shall never be put to shame." (Rom. 9:33)

- "Yet to all who received him, to those who believed in his name, he gave the right to become children of God." (John 1:12)

- "Everything is possible for him (her) who believes." (Mark 9:23)

- "We do not make requests of you because we are righteous but because of Your great mercy." (Dan. 9:18)

- "See, I have inscribed you on the palms of my hands" (Isa 49:16) and "no one can snatch (you) out of my hand." (John 10:28)

- "If anyone is in Christ he is a new creation; the old has gone, the new has come!" (2 Cor. 5:17)

(Verses from NIV)

Adoring our great God

- *"The Lord is gracious and compassionate, slow to anger and rich in love."* *(Ps. 145:8)*

- *"Great is the Lord and most worthy of praise."* *(Ps 145:3)*

- *"His anger lasts only a moment, but his favor lasts a lifetime."* *(Ps. 30:5)*

Chapter 4

Prayer-Wonders in Nature

Children and adults of all ages love a good park—trees, grass, flowers, a pond, playground equipment, ducks to feed—memories that last a lifetime.

This is where Kathi loves to take her children to just let them enjoy the space, the beauty and freedom. She tells me that she and her husband really look forward to these times with their children because during these times of exploration and discovery that are thrilling to anyone, a deep sense of awe and praise can be taught. How do you teach your children to pray prayers of praise?

This is such an important part of prayer, and so totally unnatural to the human heart. We are selfish by nature, and are not going to accidentally start praising God or anyone else. This is vital to our understanding of prayer, because the element of praise in prayer points us to the One Who alone is worthy of praise. In our prayers of praise, we are looking to Him, to adore Him because of Who He is—His qualities of love, tenderness, forgiveness, kindness, faithfulness.

It's not easy, in our busy, "instant" society, to find time to slow down, to look around us, and to enjoy the simple, yet profound things we may take for granted—a sunrise splashing across the eastern sky, announcing a new day, the wonders of the summer night sky full of bright, twinkling stars, or the delicate beauty of a daffodil.

Maybe you've heard the fictitious little story about the haughtiness of puny humans: This is a story that my niece, Teri, sent to me via the Internet. I don't know who wrote it, but it's about some scientists who got together and decided that man had come a long way and no longer needed God.

They decided to pick one outstanding scientist as their "spokesman and representative" to go to God and tell Him that they could now get along nicely without Him.

As the fable goes, the arrogant scientist walked up to God and said, "God, we've decided that we no longer need You. We're to the point that we can clone people and do many miraculous things, so we've decided we can do very well on our own."

God listened patiently and kindly to the man and after the scientist was done talking, God said, "Very well, how about this? Let's say we have a man-making contest to settle this once and for all."

To this, the arrogant scientist replied, "OK, great!"

But God added, "Now, we're going to do this just like I did back in the Garden of Eden, with Adam."

The scientist said, "Sure, no problem," and he bent down and grabbed a handful of dirt.

God just looked at him and said, "No, no, no. You don't understand. You get your own dirt!"

Our children learn from the time they are very small, that God is good, and He is not only our Creator, but He also sustains all life—moment by moment on planet Earth.

As we study His wonderful creative works—flowers,

trees, mountains, animals, and butterflies, we realize again that everything good has been put here by the hand of a loving and kind Father.

What emotions rise in your heart as you view a placid lake, or watch pelicans fishing at the beach? What do you want your child to understand about the God Who not only creates, but feeds and cares for His creatures every day?

Someone has calculated that there is no one on earth who is wealthy enough to feed all of God's creatures—even the birds, for just one day. But our powerful God provides for His birds, animals, and all of creation, every day, every week, every month, year after year.

Think of stories of nature that you can tell as you're walking with your child in the sand at the beach. There are tiny sea creatures in the tide pools, beautiful shells, little sandpipers darting back and forth looking for food each time a new wave comes in. Children, as well as adults, are fascinated by these wonders, and can grasp something new about a God who transcends everything we can understand. This is the kind of God we need—Someone Who is above our daily circumstances, Who understands, and is willing to provide, protect, and guide us.

The Master Story Teller—Christ—often used objects in nature to help to embed a profound spiritual truth. He used the visible things of nature that His listeners were most familiar with—the waving fields of grain, the farmer planting his crops, a lost lamb.

There are dramatic and mundane lessons to be drawn from nature. Some can be scary, even frightening to a child, but even from these realities of nature, there are powerful truths. And there are also stories and lessons of God's majesty and power.

Another story from e-mail is this one of a small boy

who lived in south Florida. Some years ago, as the story goes, and on a hot summer day many miles from Miami, a little boy decided to go for a swim in the old swimming hole behind his house. In a hurry to dive into the cool water, he ran out the back door, leaving behind his shoes, socks, and shirt as he went. He flew into the water, not realizing that as he swam toward the middle of the pond, an alligator was swimming toward the shore.

His mother, in the house, was looking out the window, and with mounting fear, she saw the two as they got closer and closer together. In utter terror, she ran toward the water, yelling to her son as loudly as she could. Hearing her voice, the little boy became alarmed and made a U-turn to swim to his mother. It was too late. Just as he reached her, the alligator reached him. From the dock, the mother grabbed her little boy by the arms just as the alligator snatched his legs. That began an incredible tug-of war between the two.

The alligator was much stronger than the mother, but this Mom was much too passionate to let go, and God must have strengthened her in her impossible task.

A farmer happened to drive by, heard her screams, raced from his truck, took aim, and shot the alligator. Remarkably, after weeks and weeks in the hospital, the boy survived. His legs were extremely scarred by the vicious attack of the animal. And, on his arms were deep scars where his mother's fingernails dug into his flesh in her effort to hang on to the son she loved.

The newspaper reporter who interviewed the boy after the trauma asked if he would show him his scars. The boy lifted his pants legs. And then, with obvious pride, he said to the reporter, "But look at my arms. I have great scars on my arms too. I have them because my Mom held on and wouldn't let go."

We can all identify with that boy. We have scars too. Not from an alligator, or anything quite so dramatic. But we have the scars of our past. Some of those scars are unsightly and have caused us regret. But some wounds are because God has refused to let go.

What a wonderful reality that in the midst of your struggle, He has been there holding on to you. The Scripture teaches that God loves you. He wants to protect you and provide for you in every way.

Sometimes we foolishly wade into dangerous situations. The swimming hole of life is filled with peril— and we forget that the enemy is waiting to attack. That's when the tug-of-war begins, and if you have the scars of His love on your arms, be grateful.

He did not, and will not, let you go. What a loving God we serve. What precious opportunities to instill these truths into the hearts of children.

Simple things—putting bird food out for the wild birds in your neighborhood, listening for the songs of birds, or listening to the contented purring of a kitten, or the frisky loving bark of a puppy—these are wonderful ways to be in tune with nature and to enjoy the immeasurable ways our God provides for our joy and contentment.

In the book *Patriarchs and Prophets*, we get a little glimpse into the life of a lonely shepherd boy who was startled by the unexpected call from a messenger who announced that the prophet, Samuel had come to Bethlehem and had asked for him. He was amazed to discover that he was to be anointed as the next king of Israel. But he had proven himself brave and faithful in his humble work of caring for his father's sheep and now God had chosen him for a much larger responsibility.

The ceremony of anointing David had been performed in secret, but to this youth, it was a message that God had chosen him and was marking him for his high destiny.

Even though he was given this great honor, and he knew that one day he would be given a high position, it didn't make him proud. He was just as humble as before the anointing, and he quietly returned to his sheep, content to wait for God's timing in his life. He cared for his sheep as tenderly and guarded his flocks as carefully as before.

But now his heart was even more open to learn more and more about God. With new inspiration he sang, composed his melodies, and played his harp. He enjoyed the beautiful landscape spread out before him. There were vineyards with the clusters of fruit, bright in the sunshine. He saw the trees of the forest, green and swaying in the breeze. He loved to see the sun flooding the heavens with light. He saw the bold summits of the hills reaching up toward the sky, and even though he couldn't see God, he could praise God for all of these works of His creative power.

> "Who can measure the results of those years of toil and wandering among the lonely hills? The communion with nature and with God, the care of his flocks, the perils and deliverances, the griefs and the joys, of his lowly lot, were not only to mold the character of David and to influence his future life, but through the psalms of Israel's sweet singer they were in all coming ages to kindle love and faith in the hearts of God's people, bringing them nearer to the ever-loving heart of Him in whom all His creatures live." PP 642

And David was learning lessons of trust. Moses, too was trained for his important work as he tended the sheep in Midian. So God was fitting the young boy, David, to become His guide of His chosen people. As he cared for the flocks of sheep, he was gaining an appreciation of the care that our Great Shepherd has for us—who are the sheep of His pasture.

Because he knew and trusted God, angels came to his rescue in the valley between the two mighty armies, as he and Goliath met face to face. Because God had helped him with his sheep—even when they were attacked by lions or bears, he knew that God could be trusted in any situation. And that is still true today. Our God is the same, yesterday, today, and forever.

Precious are the moments and memories spent together in nature and with the God of nature.

Some resources provide fascinating information, photographs, and can stimulate further study and growth. Check with your ABC for the Creation Journal, or something similar.

Three Parables

First Parable

I took a little child's hand in mine. He and I were to walk together for a while. I was to lead him to the Father. It was a task that overcame me, so awful was the responsibility. I talked to the little child of the Father. I painted the sternness of the Father's face were the child to displease Him. We walked under tall trees. I said the Father had power to send them crashing down, struck by His thunderbolts. We walked in the sunshine. I told him the greatness of the Father who made the burning, blazing sun.

And one twilight we met the Father. The child hid behind me, he was afraid; he would not look up at the face so loving. He remembered my picture; he would not put his hand in the Father's hand. I was between the child and the Father. I wondered. I had been so conscientious, so serious.

Second Parable

I took a little child's hand in mine. I was to lead him to the Father. I felt burdened by the multitude of things I was to teach him. We did not ramble; we hastened on from spot to spot. At one moment we compared the leaves of the different trees, in the next we were examining a bird's nest. While the child was questioning me about it, I hurried him away to chase a butterfly. Did he chance to fall asleep, I wakened him, lest he should miss something I wanted him to see. We spoke of the Father often and rapidly. I poured into his ears all the stories he ought to know. But we were interrupted often by the coming of the stars which we must needs study; by the gurgling brook which we must trace to its source.

And then in the twilight we met the Father. The child merely glanced at Him. The Father stretched out His hand, but the child was not interested enough to take it. Feverish spots burned on his cheeks. He dropped to the ground exhausted and fell asleep. Again I was between the child and the Father. I wondered. I had taught him so many, many things.

Third Parable

I took a little child's hand in mine to lead him to the Father. My heart was full of gratitude for the glad privilege. We walked slowly. I suited my steps to the short steps of the child. We spoke of the things the child noticed. Sometimes it was one of the Father's birds; we watched it build its nest, we saw the eggs that were laid. We wondered, later, at the care it gave its young.

Sometimes we picked the Father's flowers, and stroked their soft petals and loved their bright colors. Often we told stories of the Father. I told them to the child and the child told them to me. We told them, the child and I, over and over again. Sometimes we stopped to rest, leaning against the Father's tree, and letting His air cool our brows, and never speaking.

And then in the twilight we met the Father. The child's eyes shone. He looked up lovingly, trustingly, eagerly into the Father's face; he put his hand into the Father's hand. I was for the moment forgotten. I was content.

Source unknown

Personal Applications by Noelene

Ideas for Family Worship

Bring nature into family worship. Encourage your child to be on the lookout for interesting or beautiful specimens of nature that they can bring to family worship, such as leaves, feathers, flowers, fruit, pebbles, bugs, etc.

The Budding Naturalist—Adoration

Observe nature specimens with magnifying glass under bright light. Encourage the child to tell what he sees, feels, smells. Try to make with paper, scissors, glue and paint, an object similar to the natural object. Affirm the child for his efforts. Encourage him again to look at the specimen and tell what he now thinks of what God made. Get excited about God's skill as a creator. Ask: *Why did God take so much trouble to make everything so good?* (Because He wanted us to see it and say, *"Wow!"* Because He wanted to show His love for us.) Pray prayers of adoration, giving compliments to God. (God, you gave flowers a soft feel, etc.) Or praise God for Who He is (Wonderful Creator) and what He has done.

The Budding Naturalist—Thanksgiving

Explore nature as described above. Or go out into the back yard. The child and the adult each can measure off an area that is about 12 inches square. They then lie on the ground so they can see clearly the tiny creatures in the grass. Each person makes a list of the creatures or plants that they observe. Each reports their findings to the other/s. Then join hands and thank God for whatever you especially treasure from this experience.

The Budding Naturalist—Confession

Nature provides a wonderful kaleidoscope of beauty and perfection. But it also attests to decay and corruption. Challenge the kids to look in nature for signs of things that have gone wrong in our world. They might discover birds that are afraid of us, cats that stalk birds, animals that eat other creatures, bugs that destroy plants, dirt, dead flowers, etc. Be frank in discussing what is wrong in the natural world. Admit that this is not how God meant it to be. An enemy has done it. Then confess that every person, adults included, mess up sometimes. But Jesus came to fix things and make us whole. This is a great opportunity for them to welcome God into their lives.

Asking Forgiveness

Admitting that we have done wrong is never easy. But it is necessary. Encourage children to think if there is something they have done that gives them a heavy feeling inside. Encourage them to admit the problem; help them ask forgiveness. Do this whenever something has gone wrong. As a parent, remember that we should never stand in the place of the Savior. Neither are we trying to bring up children who do not need a Savior. Rather we should help children make friends with their Savior.

Praise Him Again

When children experience the difference that confession and forgiveness bring, they also experience the peace and joy that follow. They will be ready to praise God again. Make this a time to celebrate. After expressing praise, sing a praise song (God Is so Good), blow some bubbles, fly a kite or climb a tree.

Prayer and Praise Alternatives

There are more ways to pray or praise than just saying a prayer or singing. Try some of the following when you have time for a meaningful experience:

Prayer Collage

You need current newspapers or news magazines, scissors, glue, and a piece of colorful poster board (or just open out a grocery bag and iron it flat). At a table or on the floor, spread out the materials. Explain that together you are going to make a prayer poster. Cut out words and pictures and put them together to form a prayer. Words cut from headlines will look best on the poster. Where you cannot find the words you want, cut out individual letters. As the words and pictures are cut, group the messages together and glue them in order, to the poster board or brown paper. It's OK to use markers to supply missing words. When done, read the poster as a prayer. You may be surprised how current it sounds.

Prayer Grug

Gather together in a circle and pray with your eyes open. Each person thanks God for something special about the person to their left and prays for that person. Continue clockwise around the circle. The persons prayed for each time, make supplication for the person to their left. Then each person puts their arms around the shoulders of the persons next to them. Then talk a short step toward the center of the circle and hug those two people. Step forward again and hug as a group until everyone is squished.

Prayer Clock face

Make a prayer reminder by laying a dinner plate face down on a sheet of construction paper and drawing around it with a felt marker. Mark 12:00 inside the clock face and draw a vertical line down through the center to 6:00. Draw a horizontal line between 9:00 and 3:00. In each section of the clock face, the child can draw or paste a picture representing what they request prayer for at that time. They may need prayer for an afternoon class in the period between 12:00 noon and 3:00 P.M., for instance. So they draw a picture representing that class in the top right quadrant.

Supplication Search

You need a red marker and a newspaper, preferably a recent, local one. Search for and circle with red marker the stories of people in need. Discuss the basic facts. Try to imagine what the person/s involved are feeling and needing. Pray for the people by name. You might write to one of the persons or families involved. You might also want to praise God for the services of community helpers who were on the scene to help.

Texts for celebrating assurance

Quote one of the following passages to express the freedom that Jesus brings when we ask His forgiveness.

- *"Forgive and you will be forgiven."* Luke 6:3

- *"If we confess our sins, he is faithful and just and will forgive us our sins."* 1 John 1:9

- *"Whoever believes in him shall not perish, but have eternal life."* John 3:16

- *"Though your sins are like scarlet, they shall be as white as snow; though they are red as crimson, they shall be like wool."* Isa. 1:18

- *"He is able to keep you from falling and to present you ... without fault."* Jude 24.

(Verses from NIV)

Chapter 5

Big Prayers ... Little Prayers

Max Lucado tells the story of a young family sitting down to eat their evening meal together. It's just little 5-year-old Stevie, Mom, and Dad. Stevie is asked to pray, to thank Jesus for their food.

"Dear God, I hope you've had a good day. I've had a good day; thank you for the food, but God, unless Mom and Dad start talking to each other again, and fix what's wrong tonight, it's just going to be me and You having any fun. Amen."

Little prayers? Little things that come up in the course of a day. Little concerns, but there is nothing that we cannot take to God. Children soon learn what it means to talk to God about anything and everything. They see Him as a Friend and Someone Who understands.

What is a "little" prayer? What are "big" prayers? Can we tell the difference? One way to measure the size of the prayer, is to ask—"how big is the scope?" We can often see and experience the answers to the everyday, "little" prayers. Answers to the really big prayers may not be realized until eternity, but they still count. God still saves every prayer in His golden bowls in heaven (see Rev. 5:8). And these big prayers free His hands to do big things.

We need to remember the "little prayers" because God does and He answers. And we can see His answers.

Children take a promise and believe it, and often God honors their faith. We need to remember the times when God has heard and worked in wonderful ways.

Someone has said that "amnesia fosters arrogance." We need to remember. Another reason to hold on to these memories, is because it gives us faith to pray bigger and bigger prayers.

Encourage your child to think about what might be on God's heart. How would He want you to pray? Are there ways to pray for more and more of His people around the world?

What and where is the 10/40 Window?

This vast, troubled area of the earth stretches from West Africa, through the Middle East to East Asia. More than 60 countries fall within the boundaries of 10 and 40 degrees latitude north of the equator. These are the most spiritually-impoverished countries, which include the majority of Muslims, Hindus, and Buddhists in the world.

Sixty-two countries are in or touched by the 10/40 Window, and of the 6 billion people on earth, 4 billion live there.

This is where the poorest of the poor labor endlessly just to scratch out a meager existence. This is where famine has not only ravaged the land, but the minds, bodies, and spirits of the people. It is the seat where Satan has great power, and it has been called hell on earth.

How can we help children and young people reach their arms around the world? How can the peoples of the 10/40 Window be reached? How can other countries, the sleeping countries of Europe and Gospel-

Keep Praying For The People In The 10/40 Window!

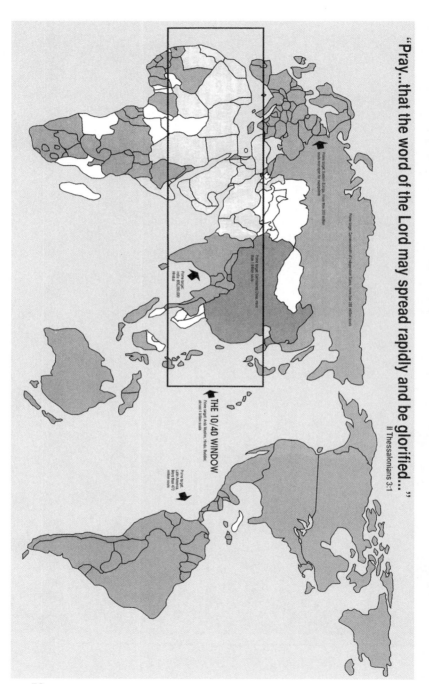

"Pray...that the word of the Lord may spread rapidly and be glorified..."
II Thessalonians 3:1

THE 10/40 WINDOW

hardened North America be awakened?

The answer to all of these questions is found in Matthew 9:37 & 38 *(NKJV)*:

> *"Then He said to His disciples, 'The harvest truly is plentiful, but the laborers are few. Therefore pray the Lord of the harvest to send out laborers into His harvest."*

This is the only place in Scripture where Christ points out an insurmountable problem, and then gives a wonderful solution. The answer is prayer.

Although we can witness to a neighbor or share our faith with a friend, most of us will never be able to visit the 10/40 window. But we can pray.

How can you teach your children to get involved in earnest intercessory prayer for these peoples in situations that seem so hopeless?

Here are a few suggestions—no doubt you'll think of others.

1. You may wish to post a map of the world in your child's room, or find a good map with the 10/40 Window to use for worship time.

2. You could use the map in this book to explain the area and need to your child.

3. You may wish to have your child meet someone who has been a missionary in one of the countries of the 10/40 Window, or invite this person to the children's Sabbath School to share stories.

4. You could use the stationery—on the next page—for a written prayer for these needy people groups. You may want to make several copies for repeated written prayers with this specific focus.

The Prayer of Jabez

There are some great prayers—big prayers—throughout Scripture. Some prayers, such as Solomon's prayer at the dedication of the temple—are long and profound. Others are short, but powerful.

The prayer of Jabez is a short, but very significant prayer, tucked away in a list of genealogies in the fourth chapter of 1 Chronicles. This is a very unlikely place to be looking for a prayer. The genealogy list is interrupted by this brief story, and then back to the lists.

> *"And Jabez called on the God of Israel saying, 'Oh, that You would bless me indeed, and enlarge my territory, that your hand would be with me, and that You would keep me from evil, that I may not cause pain!' So God granted him what he requested."*
>
> *1 Chronicles 4:10   (NKJV)*

A simple and short prayer with giant results. Many people have taken this short prayer as their own and used it daily. They've discover that God loves to hear His Word in prayer, and the prayer of Jabez becomes their own powerful prayer of faith.

1. ***Bless me indeed.*** Bless me a lot—immeasurably, and undeniably. I need you, Lord. While on others Thou art calling, don't pass me by. Some of our prayer time can and should be prayers for ourselves. It is God's nature to give and to bless. This prayer fulfills His desire to answer.

2. ***Oh, that you would enlarge my territory!*** We can live larger lives for Him. His plans are much bigger than we could ever imagine. He tells us in Ephesians 3:20, His plans are greater than we could think or ask for. He wants to enlarge, expand everything He has given us to do for Him.

3. ***Oh, that Your hand would be with me!*** It is only accomplished by His strength, His power, His wisdom. Martin Luther reminded God at the beginning of his prayer that he was human, needy, weak, helpless, and unworthy. He wants us to ask. This is a prayer for guidance.

4. ***Oh, that You would keep me from evil!*** Bruce Wilkinson says, "God will not make you great, He becomes great in and through you." He has a strategy for sustaining a blessed life. It is His protective shield around you. He wants to remove the sin that can break the cycle of abundant living and provide peace and power.

God said that Jabez was more honorable than his brothers. We don't know very much about him, except that he prayed this prayer.

Why not covenant with God to pray this prayer daily for 60 days and just see how God wants to work in your life—to bless you, to enlarge your effectiveness, to provide new power and protection.

This is a prayer, a big prayer, that children can pray with excitement and faith. Make it a daily prayer for and with them.

Biblical Strengths—to request for yourself and your children

This is a simple yet marvelous way to open Scripture praying for and with your children. Are these big prayers or little prayers? You decide. they are short prayers—but with eternal consequences. He has promised to do more *when we ask.*

1. **Salvation.** *"Lord, let salvation spring up that we may obtain the salvation that is in Christ Jesus, with eternal glory."* (Isa. 45:8, 2 Tim. 2:10)

2. **Growth in grace.** *"I pray that we may grow in the grace and knowledge of our Lord and Savior Jesus Christ."* (2 Peter 3:18)

3. **Love.** *"Grant, Lord, that we may learn to live lives of love, through the Spirit who dwells in us."* (Gal. 5:25, Eph. 5:2)

4. **Honesty and Integrity.** *"May integrity and honesty be our virtue and our protection."* (Ps. 25:21)

5. **Self Control.** *"Father, help us to be alert and self-controlled in all we do."* (1 Thess. 5:6)

6. **Love for God's Word.** *"May we grow to find Your Word more precious than much pure gold and sweeter than honey from the comb."* (Ps. 19:10)

7. **Kindness.** *"Lord, may we always try to be kind to each other and to everyone else."* (1 Thess. 5:15)

8. **Generosity.** *"Grant that we may be generous and willing to share, and so lay up treasure for ourselves as a firm foundation for the coming age."* (1 Tim.6:18, 19)

9. **Humility.** *"God, please cultivate in us the ability to show true humility toward all."* (Titus 3:2)

10. **Joy.** *"May we be filled with the joy given by the Holy Spirit."* (1 Thess. 1:6)

11. **Willingness and ability to work.** *"Teach us, Lord, to value work and to work at it with all our hearts, as working for the Lord, not for men."* (Col. 3:23)

12. **Prayerfulness.** *"Grant, Lord, that our lives will be marked by prayerfulness, that we may learn to pray in the Spirit on all occasions with all kinds of prayer and requests."* (Eph. 6:18)

13. **Passion for God.** *"Lord, please instill in us each a soul that 'followeth hard after thee' (Ps. 63:8 KJV), one that clings passionately to you."*

14. **Gratitude.** *"Help us to live lives that are always overflowing with thankfulness and always giving thanks to God the Father for everything, in the name of our Lord Jesus Christ."* (Eph. 5:20, Col. 2:7)

15. **Faith.** *"I pray that faith will find root and grow in our hearts, that by faith we may gain what has been promised to us."* (Luke 17:5,6 & Heb. 11: 1-40)

(Verses paraphrased from NIV)

Personal Applications by Noelene

A Parent's Jabez Prayer

Lord, make me not afraid or slow to ask of You:
"Bless me a lot."

Extend my Christian influence
In a child's life and in her world.

Keep me dependent on You;
keep the devil at bay.

Don't let me hurt a little one
or be a stumbling block.

Thank You for granting my request.

Understanding a Child's Growth in Prayer

A small child will not understand a Jabez prayer, nevertheless his little prayer, spoken from his heart can be profound. Not only do prayers grow in grace as the child grows in favor with God and with other people, but their little prayers, by God's grace, grow the person—spiritually.

Children's prayers are meant to grow and mature with their minds. But sadly, some grow into young adulthood with their prayers lagging behind at an elementary level.

When teaching children to petition God, consider the following:

Preschool children ...

- *Want immediate answers to concrete requests,*

- *Live in a small world—home, church, neighborhood,*

- *Pray for what they see.*

So they pray for . . .

- *Immediate, inconsequential concerns, such as: pets, toys, objects in nature; "Thank you for ... "*

- *People they know; "God bless ... ,"*

- *People on TV shows, characters in their picture books (maybe even Pooh Bear and Tigger!).*

Lower elementary children are ...

- *Learning to wait for what they want,*

- *Aware of a wider world through TV news and church news,*

- *Curious about other countries and peoples.*

So they can learn to petition for . . .

- *Bigger concerns—unconverted relatives, neighbors, missionaries, the pastor*

- *People in the news, people in crisis, those who are sick*

- *People in other countries*

Older elementary children ...

- *Reason from cause to effect*

- *Are knowledgeable about the wider world*

- *Are empathetic to victims of tragedy and disaster*

So help them petition for . . .

- *People affected by war, disasters, evil;*

- *The conversion of their neighbors; the alleviation of suffering in global hot spots,*

- *Un-reached people groups; ministries like Adventist Development and Relief Agency, Adventist World Radio, and Maranatha International that serve people in other countries*

More Prayer Activities for the Family

1. ***Prayer posters.*** Talk to the family about little and big prayers. Make two posters, one small and one big. Write little family prayer requests on the small one and big requests on the larger one. Cut and paste pictures from the newspaper of countries/ disasters that you are praying for. Perhaps write a prayer for them.

2. ***Prayer maps.*** Purchase or make a world map. Highlight or circle countries that you have read about in the newspaper and are praying for. Decorate the edges with pictures of people from those countries that you cut from newspapers.

3. ***Prayer album.*** Include photographs of people for whom you are praying. Write beneath the photo the name of the person/persons and what specifically you are asking for them. Add a Bible promise that you are claiming for them. Talk about God's memory and the place in it for each of you. Thank the Lord that He does not forget you or your prayer concerns. The Holy Spirit pleads in anguish for those we are praying for.

4. ***God's prayer request.*** Petition God to know what big prayer request is on His mind. As family members pray for God's concerns; write them in your prayer journal, album, or poster.

5. ***Prayer walk.*** Walk around your neighborhood as a family (that may be parent and child), praying for the people who live in the houses on your street or block. Ask the Holy Spirit to move on their hearts so that they will come to Jesus. If you cannot actually walk the neighborhood, drive it, map it, and pray as if you are out there.

6. ***Doorway prayers.*** Read Ex. 12:13, 21-23. Walk through your house thinking about the fathers sprinkling the blood on all the doorposts. Pray that the blood of Jesus, which has the power to save, will be over all who enter these rooms, so that your house will be a refuge, a hiding place, from the evil one.

7. ***Global mission prayers.*** Watch in the *Adventist Review* or other mission magazine for articles about unreached people groups or stories about missionaries. Or look for the lists of student missionaries going out from your country. Add to your prayer poster the names you read about. Pray for some of these peoples and individuals every day.

Chapter 6

Family Summits

The commonly accepted definition of a "summit", is a meeting of leaders. So when you have family worship, call together your leaders and potential leaders to hear God's voice, His instruction to you personally. He says to you in *The Living Bible*, in Proverbs 1: 5 & 6:

"I want those already wise to become wiser and become leaders by exploring the depths of meaning in these nuggets of truth. How does a man become wise? The first step is to trust and reverence the Lord."

My husband has always loved the book of Proverbs. We have taken this book for family worship—as a focus for family discussion and prayer. When Jerry and Randy were teenagers, in the evening we often took one chapter, reading it slowly and thoughtfully, then sharing our thoughts and impressions before our prayers. There's a chapter for each day of the month.

Former Senator John Ashcroft (R-Missouri) has a devotional time each morning at 8 AM in his office with his staff. They call it RAMP—they read a Scripture passage, "argue about it," memorize Scripture, and pray together. The Senator said, "We could have used another word instead of "argue," but it didn't make a word!" Their sharing is encouraging and meaningful. Their prayers are personal and specific.

As you come together to put the hands of your children into His Almighty hand, you are given an infallible guidebook. Here are a just a few references:

His faithfulness and willingness to help:

> *"The Lord will not forsake his people, for they are his prize."* Psalm 94:14 TLB

> God's Word teaches His people *"how to act in every circumstance, for he wanted them to be understanding, just and fair in everything they did."* Proverbs. 1:2,3 TLB

> *"God has given sacred promises; no wonder I exult!"* Psalm 108:7 TLB

> *"God is with you, he protects you.* Proverbs 3:26 TLB

Knowing and following Jesus:

> *"If you want favor with both God and man, and a reputation for good judgment and common sense, then trust the Lord completely; don't ever trust yourself. In everything you do, put God first, and he will direct you and crown your efforts with success."* Proverbs 3: 4-6 TLB

> *"Reverence for God adds hours to each day."* Proverbs 10:27 TLB

Importance of wisdom:

> *"Have two goals: wisdom—that is, knowing and doing right—and common sense. Don't let them slip away, for they fill you with living energy, and are a feather in your cap."* Proverbs 3:21, 22 TLB

> *I, wisdom, will make the hours of your day more profitable and the years of your life more fruitful."* Proverbs 9:11 TLB

Relationships:

"But the good man walks along in the ever-brightening light of God's favor; the dawn gives way to morning splendor, while the evil man gropes and stumbles in the dark."   Proverbs 4:18 TLB

"Above all else, guard your affections. For they influence everything else in your life."   Proverbs 4:23 TLB

"Be with wise men and become wise. Be with evil men and become evil."   Proverbs 13:20 TLB

Attitudes

"Your own soul is nourished when you are kind; it is destroyed when you are cruel."   Proverbs 11:17 TLB

"To learn, you must want to be taught. To refuse reproof is stupid.   Proverbs 12:1 TLB

Financial guidance:

"It is possible to give away and become richer! It is also possible to hold on too tightly and lose everything.
                                                            Proverbs 11:24 TLB

"Trust in your money and down you go! Trust in God and flourish as a tree."   Proverbs 11:28 TLB

"It is better to get your hands dirty—and eat, than to be too proud to work—and starve."   Proverbs 12:9 TLB

Tongue control:

"Some people like to make cutting remarks, but the words of the wise soothe and heal."   Proverbs 12:18 TLB

"Self control means controlling the tongue! A quick retort can ruin everything."   Proverbs 13:3 TLB

"Keep your mouth closed and you'll stay out of trouble."
                                                            Proverbs 21:23 TLB

Obedience:

"Despise God's Word and be in trouble. Obey it and succeed."   Proverbs 13:13 TLB

"If you refuse to discipline your son, it proves you don't love him; for if you love him you will be prompt to punish him."   Proverbs 13;24 TLB

"Don't envy evil men but continue to reverence the Lord all the time, for surely you have a wonderful future ahead of you. There is hope for you yet."
                                        Proverbs 23:17, 18 TLB

My friend, Dick Eastman, a writer and speaker in the field of prayer, tells a story of his children, and the impact of Scripture on their lives. At this time in his ministry, he was a youth pastor, and involved in leading large groups of young people in a Prayer Ministry they called the "Gap" Ministry. The idea was based on the text in Ezekiel 22:30:

I sought for a man among them who would make a wall, and stand in the gap before me on behalf of the land, that I should not destroy it: but I found no one."

Groups of young people began what they called the GAP MINISTRY praying for the world—continent by continent, including all people groups.

Dick's two little daughters were about 4 and 6 when someone gave them a three-story doll house for Christmas—with all the little furniture complete with little "Barbie" dolls, which they loved.

After one of his ministry trips, his wife, Dee, had an interesting sight to show him. She took him back to their daughter, Ginger's room, and there beside the doll house was a place for prayer—a separate little place in the "garden" near the doll house. Dick and

Dee were living in the Sacramento, California, area at the time, and he had a special place in their back yard which he used as his prayer place.

She said that she overheard the children playing with their dolls, and speaking for them, and she heard one of the "Barbie" dolls say to the other one, well, I'll have to go now, I have to have my "Gap" time.

The other dolly answered (with the help of Ginger's little sister) "OK, have a nice prayer time." So the little Barbie doll pranced out to her place for prayer.

As Dick was telling the story, he said, "You might think, by the way they dress, that they are reprobates, but I can tell you that some of these Barbie dolls are saved!"

But that wasn't all. After another trip, she again took him to the doll house to see the latest developments. The girls had rounded up all their dollies, and anyone else's they could find, and they were out playing somewhere, but l the dollies were having a prayer meeting. The "Gap" space had been enlarged, and it was now larger than the doll house. There was a big prayer meeting, and the dollies were kneeling—some looked like their little knees had been coerced into that position, but it was a big prayer meeting.

No one had said anything to the little girls about this. They had "picked it up" as they observed what was going on in their environment. The Holy Spirit uses any influence to reach our children. What opportunities are we providing for this divine work? The Lord takes something we thought was inconsequential, and makes something meaningful from it in the lives of our children and grandchildren.

Family prayer time is a very special time of closeness and intimacy. Praying together brings people closer. Make these family worship times happy and short.

Leave family members wanting more and guessing what will happen next.

Children can participate at their level of understanding and ability. Here is where the principles learned from the experiences of their day can be shared, emphasized, and enjoyed.

Children can be given respect and value as you point out to them, in their family setting, how you see God at work in their lives. Our children crave and need "the blessing." This is an affirmation that God is using them in specific ways, because He had a purpose for each one when He gave us life. Point out to them that they are valued in heaven, and in this circle.

Someone has said that for every negative experience we need 20 positive experiences just to offset it—because the scolding, or the embarrassment or negative input experienced is so much stronger in our minds.

The "blessing" from parents, friends, and teachers is a precious experience that brings hope, healing, and new direction.

Jacob wanted a blessing, the spiritual birthright that was promised. He couldn't wait for God's timing, so he missed that special experience. Because he and his mother connived and worked around God's plan, Jacob suffered all of his life. He became known as someone who couldn't be trusted. He, himself was treated this way, until he came to a crisis in his life—at the brook Jabbock. When Jacob discovered Who it was he was wrestling with, he was determined that he wouldn't miss the blessing this time. He needed it too much.

He said, "I will not let you go until you bless me." Here was his finest moment. He would not let it slip away without the blessing he had wanted all his life.

God did bless him. He changed his name. He changed his life—his character, that early morning at the brook. From then on, Jacob became the true father of the nation of Israel. He blessed his own children, his grandchildren, and even blessed Pharaoh (Genesis 47:10).

God wants to bless us. He wants to change our name, our life—if we are willing. If you're feeling insecure, He wants to bring His strength and peace. If you need faith, He supplies His faithfulness. He covers us with the blood of Jesus and cleanses. This changes our lives.

We can pass this marvelous experience of blessing on to our children. It is simple, but has a tremendous impact on their hearts and lives.

When doing this blessing, select one child at a time. first, point out how you see God at work in that child's life. Let each one in the circle contribute their words of appreciation and affirmation.

Then put an arm around that shoulder, or hold them in a hug as you pray a special prayer asking for God's Spirit to work a very special work in this precious life. Thank God for this child, and let your children know that they are loved and appreciated—in heaven, and in your home.

Then let them participate in giving the blessing to others in the family. There is such a special experience in giving and receiving the blessing.

In other family worship times you may want to use symbols that teach them about God and how to talk to Him. Help them to visualize and experience in as many ways as possible. This makes learning a fun experience.

Solomon said that a "wise teacher makes learning a joy." Times of family worship can be a joy. And we remember the things that we experience longer than just a message that is spoken. Think about the possibilities—just in using the senses in helping children experience truths about God and prayer:

VISUAL—There is an endless array of nature objects, shells, sunsets, sunrises, birds, trees, flowers. Teach them to really see more than the obvious.

Help them to visualize. As you tell stories, help them to visualize stories of the gospels, to use their imagination and put themselves right into each story.

TASTE—If you are telling the story of the woman at the well, let them drink some cool water. Talk about the thirst of Jesus, and the woman, and living water. If you are talking about the Psalms, you may wish to give them some honey, as you talk about what David says about "honey from the rock."   (Psalm 81:16)

They'll love tasting different kinds of grapes as you tell the story of the spies in Canaan, and explain the enormous size of the grapes then. Or let them taste olive oil as you talk about how it was used then and now.

TOUCH—Think of ways that you can let them "feel" something that will illustrate what you are talking about. Maybe it will be the lambswool, or a very soft fabric, to illustrate softness and kindness and how good it feels. Let them feel flowers and objects of nature as you explain and answer their questions.

HEARING—An important and sometimes neglected part of personal and family prayer is music. Sing songs that are appropriate for the ages of the children. Let them choose the songs. Use some songs as prayers, and let them close their eyes and sing these songs to Jesus.

Use other sound effects when telling Bible stories, sounds of animals, birds, thunder claps. You have a drum in your kitchen cabinet. Just turn a pot upside down, and use a wooden spoon as a drum stick, or cover the spoon with a washcloth. Use a trumpet when you're telling the story of Jericho. There are resources at your fingertips.

SMELL—As you're teaching them a new thought, or wanting to reinforce a truth from Scripture, use the fragrance of flowers or the sweet smells of a fresh orange, apple, or banana. Try using cedar, or other woods. Whatever is appropriate and illustrates your theme can be better remembered when the senses are brought into the learning experience.

Personal Applications by Noelene

Group Prayer Experiences

Whether you are praying with a partner, with the whole family, or leading a prayer group or large class, group prayer can be an exciting experience. The group will be drawn closer to God and to each other as a result. And any fear of unpleasant, guilt-dominating prayer meetings will vanish.

To conduct a group prayer experience you need to choose the type of prayer you will pray and fit it to the needs of those involved. Group prayer is not something to do on the spot without preparation, unless it is thrust on you at the last minute. If you know ahead, pray and plan with the Holy Spirit to guide you.

Planning a group prayer experience. Ask the Holy Spirit to create a sweet, trusting atmosphere of prayer where nobody is trying to pull rank with God or put someone else down. Then prayerfully select a type of prayer that your group will enjoy. Seek a Bible passage to read either before the prayer or as a basis for the prayer. If you need help in selecting a passage, try one of the passages we have suggested below.

For certain results, especially in tense situations, pray that the Lord will push back the powers of darkness that press in to prevent God's blessing. This is one prayer that God never fails to answer instantly. Having a group in another room praying separately for the success of your prayer group also brings added power. The fervent prayers of righteous people truly do avail much.

The first time your group tries praying as a group, you may want to make a short explanation or the procedure, such as the following:

1. What is prayed here, stays here. We treat the prayers of others with confidentiality.

2. We can be open and honest with God. Nobody has to prove anything to the group. We are not praying for the benefit of anyone but God.

3. There are three ways you can take part:

   a. By praying one or two sentences in your own words.

   b. By starting to sing a hymn appropriate to the prayer. Everyone will join in.

   c. By quoting scripture appropriate to the prayer.

4. We are all equals when we kneel at the foot of the cross. Every prayer is precious. We can affirm each other's prayers with a heartfelt "amen" or by saying, "Yes, Lord" or by praying, "Lord, I want to affirm (name's) prayer for" (be specific; add a sentence of prayer for that person).

5. I will guide the prayer so that we enter into it as a group.

Types of group prayer

The ACTS prayer. An ACTS prayer is based on the acronym: Adoration, Confession, Thanksgiving, and Supplication. At the start of the prayer group, explain the acronym and write it on the board to cue the group. If an ACTS prayer is new to people, you might want to read an ACTS prayer that you have written yourself, something like the following:

Dear God,

Adoration: We open our hears in praise because we want to adore You. You have made us. You know us. You have told us that "the eternal God is our refuge and underneath are (Your) everlasting arms."

Confession: We confess our great need of you. Lord, we are ashamed of our faultfinding and lack of love. We need Your forgiveness and love.

Thanksgiving: Thank You for forgiveness and for lifting us up to start over. Thank you for the blessings of your grace; we are undeserving but you heap us with blessing anyway. Thank you, Heavenly Father.

Supplication: We ask you today for healing for our broken hearts. Please make us channels of your grace. Lead our families to know you more fully. Amen.

Leading an ACTS prayer. When leading an ACTS prayer, remind the group of the procedure and then kneel to pray. The prayer leader will do the following:

1. Start the prayer, saying something like this: "Father, we bow together as a group because you have promised that where one or two are gathered to pray that you are in the midst of them."

2. Pray a very short prayer of praise and adoration and start singing, "Oh, come let us adore Him" from the carol, "Oh, Come all Ye Faithful." Wait for the group to offer their prayers of adoration. You might want to suggest that this is a time to tell God what you appreciate about Him. Children will understand it as giving God compliments.

3. Say: "Lord, we confess our need of you." Add a sentence or two of confession and then wait for others to pray. (Confession is hard to pray in public; so you might suggest that everyone silently tell God what they have done that they are sorry about.) End the confession by singing to the same two lines of the carol used during adoration: "Forgive us, Lord, we pray You (3 times). Amen."

4. Similarly introduce thanksgiving and Supplication (asking God for help for themselves and others).

Popcorn Prayers. are spontaneous one-word or one-sentence prayers—usually following a certain theme—with everyone participating at random, or someone directs the prayer.

Scripture Prayers. Scripture prayers take a passage and divide it up into parts, as it seems appropriate for the group and for a fulfilling prayer experience. Look for a place to stop and praise God with adoration, confess your need, petition God for others, and thank Him for on-going blessings, though you need not use those terms, and they may not fall naturally in that order. The following is a Scripture prayer based on Matthew 21.

Scripture on which to base a group prayer

As you do your daily Bible reading, be on the lookout for passages that lend themselves to meaningful prayers. Whether you use them with a group or enjoy them yourself, look for special meaning for you in the passage and stop to pray about each insight you receive. To get you started on Scriptural prayers, we suggest that you try one of the following passages:

1. ***The Lord's Prayer.*** Matt. 6: 9-15. Pray about key words, such as "Father" and "hallowed" (holy). And about ideas, such as: "your kingdom come."

2. ***Mary's Song.*** Luke 1:46-55. Read and pray as follows: 46-47—Adoration, 48-49— thanksgiving, 50—supplication, 51-53—confession, 54-55— Thanksgiving and supplication again.

3. **Zachariah's Song**. Matt. 1:68-79. 68-71—Praise God; 72-75—Confess our breaking of the covenant; 76-77—Thanksgiving for Jesus, forgiveness, and salvation; 78-79—Supplication for those in spiritual darkness or in distress.

4. **A Parent's Prayer**. 2 John. Verse 3—Praise to God for His grace; 4—Thanksgiving for children who are faithful; 5-6—Confession of disobedience and lack of love; 7-12—Supplication for children based on these verses.

5. **Prayer of the Faithful**. Heb. 10 selected texts. 19-22, first part—praise for confidence in Jesus; 22—confession of guilt; 23-25—thanksgiving and supplication for each other; 35-36—thanksgiving for confidence of Jesus' return.

6. **Family Blessing**. Ps. 20. Verses 1-3—confession of need; 4-5—petition; 6—praise for the God who saves; 7-8 thanksgiving for God's blessings.

7. **Pray a Psalm**. The following Psalms make complete and rewarding prayers: 8, 19, 23, 27, 40 (select verses), 51, 90:1-12.

Chapter 7

We're all children

"My son Paul, is six," a young pastor told me recently, "and it is getting harder and harder to just 'hold' him. He wants to be active and doing things. He loves to show me what he's learned, and he doesn't like to just 'nestle' in my arms like he used to. But sometimes when he gets really tired, he'll relax and fall asleep in my arms or on my shoulder, and I get to revel in the closeness again."

Then he said, "That's the way we are with God. He wants to hold you, to hear about the little things in your life, to have you stop and listen and wait to hear His voice. We want to be rushing about for Him, to show Him that we are working for Him."

Corrie ten Boom used to say—"Don't wrestle, nestle." Nestle in His arms, relax, believe, trust.

God's blessing through Moses to the children of Israel had one very amazing promise for the little tribe of Benjamin. It's a short blessing, but packed into it is an almost unbelievable promise: *"He shall dwell between the shoulders of God."*

What an incredible thought! What a promise! Where are you, if you're between His shoulders? One theologian described that as being cradled on His breast. He is holding you lovingly in His arms and close to His heart. The *SDA Commentary* says that this could mean that you are being carried on His shoulders. No matter, either picture is one of closeness with our God. No wonder His invitations time after time throughout

Scripture are calls to intimacy with Him, the God of the universe!

And He says to you and me—"I really love you. Trust me. Get to really know Me intimately."

He is holding you in His arms or on His shoulders. And He tells you that you are the "apple," the most protected part of the eye. He really likes you.

You may say, "Father, You seem so far away."

Hear His reply: "No, I'm right here, and I will never leave you nor forsake you." He longs for closeness with us. He wants to hold us, to have us depend on Him.

One of the most valuable assets that Joshua possessed was the realization of his own inadequacy, and his need for dependence on his Father. Many times throughout the book of Joshua you can hear God saying to him, "Be strong!"

And He says that to us as parents, as teachers. "I have a work for you to do, and I'll be with you." Joshua was humble in his own eyes, but not distrustful of God's power and His promises. He didn't depend on himself, his own wisdom or his own strength. He knew he was not sufficient for the task that lay ahead. But over and over God said to him, and He says the same to you and me: "Take courage, never fear or be dismayed!"

You didn't get a diploma or certificate that says "YOU QUALIFY AS A PARENT." No one took you through the ropes and taught you—you didn't get this at graduation, and your parents didn't either. We learn and grow, realizing our inadequacies. We can turn to our heavenly Father, Who is not only the Eternal God, but also wants, as Paul tells us, to be our "Dad," and closer than a brother.

My husband has often said that there is no more profound message in all the world than this little hymn—
Jesus Loves Me. Maybe we need to sing it now and
then, and let it's deep, powerful, and soothing message
permeate our souls.

Jesus loves me, this I know, for the Bible tells me so.

*Little ones to Him belong; they are weak, but He is
strong.*

*Yes, Jesus loves me. Yes, Jesus loves me. Yes, Jesus loves
me,*

The Bible tells me so.

When He has to turn from those in the judgment, it
will be those who have been busily working for Him,
who tell Him all they have done.

*"Many will say to Me in that day, 'Lord, Lord, have we not
prophesied in Your name, cast out demons in Your name,
and done many wonders in Your name?"*
*And then I will declare to them, 'Depart from Me, I never
knew you'. ... "*

A pastor explained that passage this way, "That means
that He is saying, 'I didn't know you intimately. We
never really got acquainted. You didn't ask My advice,
you didn't want My counsel. You didn't come to Me
with all the little things in your life.' "

He wants us to know Him intimately, and to walk with
Him in obedience. He treasures that. He values your
thoughts and words, your ideas and goals. Because He
is our Parent, He enjoys us. He says that *"He rejoices
over us with singing."*   Zephaniah 3:17

And that's like our Father. What a sobering thought.
He really likes you. Children can grasp this. Children
are eager to trust and they just believe that they can

rest "between His shoulders."

And because we are His children, we can too. No wonder Jesus said that we must become as little children—trusting, willing to relax and rest in His arms, willing to be held close. We are, after all, His children. I don't want God to ever have to say about me, as the young pastor said about his son, Paul, at the beginning of this chapter, ... "It's getting harder and harder to just hold him/her. He/she wants to be active and doing things ... " I want to truly learn to nestle, next to His heart.

Personal Applications by Noelene

Intimate with Jesus

Helping children understand intimacy

Being intimate is like being very good friends. Very good friends spend time together and trust each other implicitly. Intimate friends act out of love and respect for each other; they don't mind changing their plans to accommodate the other person.

Little children are naturally intimate. When Jesus said, "except you become as little children," what did He have in mind? Ellen White says, "The simplicity and self forgetfulness, and the confiding love of a little child are the attributes that heaven values" (*Desire of Ages*, 422). These three factors are foundational to intimacy with God.

We are also told that "the strongest and noblest characters are built on the foundation of patience, love, and submission to God's will" (*Acts of the Apostles*, 319). Are these come from intimacy with God.

Chapters 7-9 of *Desire of Ages* paint a picture of Jesus' intimacy with God through childhood and adolescence. His example provides a role model for our children today. Consider the following ideas from *Desire of Ages:*

1. Mary *"through the Holy Spirit ... received wisdom to cooperate with the heavenly agencies in the development of this child."* (p. 43)

2. *"The experience which is obtained through a personal acceptance of God's word"* was more important than learning in the schools of the rabbis. (p. 44)

3. Students of the rabbis *"did not hear (God's) voice speaking to the heart."* (Ibid.)

4. As Jesus advanced from childhood to youth, *"God was His instructor."* (Ibid.)

5. "He lived to bless others. For this He found resources in nature." (p.46).

6. Satan *"left no means untried to ensnare Jesus. No child of humanity will ever be called to live a holy life amid so fierce a conflict with temptation as was our Savior."* (p. 47)

7. *"In His industrious life there were no idle moments to invite temptation."* (Ibid.)

8. *"Jesus did not shirk care and responsibility."* (p. 48)

9. *"It is in His home life that He is the pattern for all children and youth."* (p. 50)

10. In the temple at age 12, Jesus *"witnessed the impressive rites of the paschal service. Day by day He saw their meaning more clearly. Every act seemed to be bound up with His own life."* (p. 53)

11. At the temple Jesus assumed that His work was now at the temple. But when His parents remonstrated with Him, He *"hid in His own heart the mystery of His mission, waiting submissively for the appointed time ... to enter upon His work."*

12. From an early age *"Jesus had begun to act for Himself in the formation of His character"* (61). Now increasingly he found himself at odds with His brothers and with the religious leaders. *"His strict obedience to the law of God they condemned as stubbornness."* (Ibid.)

13. *"His hours of happiness were found when alone with nature and with God." "The early morning*

often found Him in some secluded place, meditating, searching the Scriptures, or in prayer." (65)

14. *"From these quiet hours He would return to His home to take up His duties again, and to give an example of patient toil."* (Ibid.)

As your children grow

Help them listen to God's voice talking to them; do the following:

- Keep describing to them the life of Jesus.

- Simplify the ideas from *Desire of Ages* and add them as details to your story.

- Teach them to memorize Scripture.

- Ask them what God is trying to tell them through the stories and verses that they study.

- When older children ask you for advice, ask them if they have asked God about their problem. And if they have, ask them to state what they think God is telling them.

- Try to help children find a Biblical principal on which to base their decisions.

- Help older children keep a journal of the lessons they are learning or the helpful texts they are finding.

Texts that Jesus lived by

The following texts helped the boy Jesus withstand temptation, according to *Desire of Ages*, pp. 64-65:

- Ps. 119:1-3
- Job 28:28
- Ps. 119: 9, 11
- Ps. 119:14-1
- Prov. 3:1-4

Appendix

The Triumphal Entry—A prayer for a group of children or adults

Preparation—Praying from Scripture can be a powerful experience. Children and adults take their prayers to God, with their worship, needs, thanksgiving and petitions, using this method of prayer. You'll find a new depth in prayer using God's Word.

What is the focus? Is this in your home, school, church, Sabbath School? Who will be participating? What are some of the general and specific needs?

The goal of the Triumphal Entry directed prayer time may be to reach out to others; it could also be used when praying for healing for families, homes, and other groups.

Introduction—Explain briefly what will be done. One person will be reading the Scripture, and pointing out a specific prayer emphasis with each verse. In a large group, divide into smaller units for prayer, with no more than 3 or 4 in each group. Invite them to pray a short prayer so that all can contribute each time— maybe just sentence prayers.

As you begin the prayer time, a short song would be appropriate, acappella. Choose a song that the children know—"*Into My Heart*," or "*Come, Holy Spirit*," etc.

Matthew 21—selected verses (Taken from the *International Children's Bible*)

> Verse 8 - *"Many people spread their coats on the road before Jesus. Others cut branches from the trees and spread them on the road.*
>
> Verse 9 - *Some of the people were walking ahead of Jesus. Others were walking behind him. All the people were shouting,*
>> *'Praise to the Son of David!*
>> *God bless the One Who comes in the name of the Lord!*
>> *Praise to God in heaven!'*

(You may wish to lead the group in singing a praise chorus here, or the Doxology, or similar song).

Ask the group to pray short, sentence prayers of PRAISE only, welcoming Jesus as the crowd did, praising Him for Who He is, for His character, for the kind of God He is.

(Now pause and give them enough time to do this).

> Verse 6 - *"The followers went and did what Jesus told them to do."*
>
> Verse 7 - *"They brought the donkey and the colt to Jesus. They laid their coats on the donkey and Jesus sat on them."*

Jesus' followers (disciples) did exactly what Jesus told them to do. They may not have understood everything, but they obeyed. Let's pray now, short prayers, asking God to give us obedient hearts, to hear His voice and to obey exactly.

(Allow time for prayer).

Verse 10 - "Then Jesus went into Jerusalem. The city was filled with excitement. The people asked, 'Who is this?' "

Verse 11 - "The crowd answered, 'This man is Jesus. The is the prophet from the town of Nazareth in Galilee.' "

The whole city was excited. (Some versions say that Jerusalem was moved, stirred). Let's pray that our hearts will be excited, and moved, that our families and our churches will be stirred and moved and excited. Let's ask God to awaken us to realize Who He is and what He can do.

(Allow time for prayer).

Before reading the next verse, to close off this part of the prayer time, you could begin singing a song like, *"Jesus, Jesus, Jesus, There's Just Something About That Name."*

Verse 12 - "Jesus went into the temple. He threw out all the people who were buying and selling there. He turned over the tables that belonged to the men who were exchanging different kinds of money. And he upset the benches of those who were selling doves."

Verse 13 - "Jesus said to all the people there, 'It is written in the Scriptures, My temple shall be a house where people will pray. But you are changing God's house into a hideout for robbers."

Pray now that God will cleanse our heart temple, our family, our church, school and community, and make our lives and churches true temples of worship, where people will pray,and where He will be seen and given glory and honor.

(Allow time for prayer).

An appropriate song here might be "*In My Life, Lord, Be Glorified,*" or "*Have Thine Own Way, Lord.*"

> *Verse 14 - "The blind and crippled people came to Jesus in the Temple, and Jesus healed them."*

Pray that God will make our lives, our families, and our churches places for true healing, to bring hope and encouragement to others.

Pray that we will have kindness and love for those around us who do not know Jesus.

(Allow time to pray).

> *Verse 22 - "If you believe, you will get anything you ask for in prayer."*

Close this time of prayer with praise. He is a big God. These are His promises. Let's ask Him for greater and greater faith, for more praise, for victory, for greater love, and that our lives and churches will be filled with praise and gratitude.

(Allow time for a closing prayer, then a song, and end with a general prayer, and pray for each individual in the group, that God will do miraculous things in each life).